Series Editor: Brian H Edwards

Day One

TRAVEL WITH

Travel with John Calvin

Geneva's minister whose thinking changed the world

CONTENTS

 First printed 2009

A CIP record is held at The British Library ISBN 978-1-84625-131-3

Published by Day One Publications Ryelands Road, Leominster, HR6 8NZ

01568 613 740 FAX 01568 611 473 email: sales@dayone.co.uk www.dayone.co.uk

Design: studiohope limited, www.studiohope.co.uk Printed by Polskabook, Poland

IOHANNES · CALVINV

ANNO · ÆTATIS · 53 ·

· B ·

Meet John Calvin

Calvin may not seem the ideal travel companion because of his reputation for being austere and forbidding. However, a little closer acquaintance makes the idea of journeying with him more appealing. For one thing he travelled in some very pleasant places. Born in Noyon in northern France, Calvin travelled around much of France, visited a friend in Italy and can be found in various German and Swiss cities. However, he is most associated with Geneva, from where his influence spread across Europe and beyond.

More significantly, what happened in these pleasant places is of continuing importance. Equipped with an excellent education, Calvin was deeply influenced by the new thinking in the sixteenth century that taught people to rediscover the true message of the Bible. During his university studies Calvin became a sincere Christian, and although his desire was to be an academic, God had other plans. A 'chance' meeting in Geneva changed the course of his life and Calvin reluctantly agreed to stay and lead the reformation there. People from across Europe came and saw what he was doing, and as young pastors and evangelists returned to Calvin's homeland his influence spread.

Calvin wrote letters to leaders and ordinary people, many suffering for their faith, but he was also a prolific author, and his *Institutes of the Christian Religion* and commentaries on the Bible made his name famous. His preaching and lecturing brought hundreds of young men to learn from his clarity and wisdom.

Today we live with the positive legacy of his achievements as we do with few others, and we can uncover Calvin as a man—both his strengths and his weaknesses. He is a good travelling companion, whether you visit some of the places he knew, or travel his road of faith through, as he himself expressed it, 'the labyrinth' of this world to the eternal city of God.

Facing page: *John Calvin in early middle age.*

1 Ordinary childhood, extraordinary student

Born in a quiet French provincial city, John Calvin studied hard in Paris where he moved in circles sympathetic to the new learning and reform of the church. His ambition was for a life devoted to quiet study but the ideas sown as seeds in his youth would change the church and the world in years to come

John Calvin was born on 10 July 1509 in the small city of Noyon, about 90 km (56 mi) northeast of Paris. The city itself has a magnificent cathedral that made it an ecclesiastical centre as well as a centre for commerce and government. The surrounding region is known as Picardy, and although not the most picturesque area of France, its land is fertile which made it relatively prosperous in Calvin's time. The area has sadly suffered much from wars. Later in life Calvin made one of his few references to his childhood when lamenting the destruction of the city by the Spanish, and more recently in the 20th century Noyon suffered severe destruction during the First World War. Among the buildings that were destroyed was the house in which Calvin was born.

Calvin's father Gerard and his mother Jeanne moved to the original house in Noyon at some point before his birth. That they did so was a sign of Gerard's success since moving. The family name was Cauvin which was later changed to the Latinized 'Calvin'. Traditionally the Cauvins were boatmen and coopers, but Gerard had greater ambitions than navigating boats on the River Oise and so, as a young man he moved from the nearby village of Pont d'Evêque to Noyon. At Noyon, through his administrative ability, he rose in local government and became a registrar of the city and an administrator and solicitor to the diocese. Gaining wealth and respectability he married Jeanne le Franc, the daughter of a relatively well off innkeeper. By 1489 Gerard applied for and was admitted to the bourgeoisie

Facing page: *The ancient cathedral library in Noyon*
Right: *An old view of Noyon*

Dr.L.H.Lee

of the city and became in time a member of the city council. Gerard Cauvin had arrived.

We know little about Jeanne Cauvin. Sadly she died before any of the five sons reached maturity, but she seems to have been a very devout woman. Years later, in his *Treatise on Relics*, Calvin recalled being taken by her to the nearby Abbey of Ourskamp, about 6 km from Noyon. Today the abbey is a ruin, but when Calvin was a child it was a significant place of pilgrimage. On his visit John remembered being allowed to kiss a fragment of the hand of St Ann. Jeanne died in 1515 when Calvin was six, and his father remarried, but we know nothing about John's stepmother or what influence, if any, she had on him. Of Jeanne and Gerard's five sons only three reached adulthood. All of them were baptized in the Church of Sainte Godeberte opposite their parents' house. Charles became a priest and

Photo by SO Leblanc

Top left: *The church in Pont l'Evêque*
Top right: *Calvin's birthplace as reconstructed on the original site. The original building was destroyed in the First World War*
Above: *The Cathedral in Noyon*

Above: *The Cathedral cloister in Noyon*
Below: *The Cathedral in Noyon that Calvin would have known as a child*

later quarrelled with the local religious authorities, but Antoine came to share John's evangelical faith and followed him to Geneva. Gerard also had two daughters by his second wife. One of them, Marie, also came to live in Geneva where she married and settled.

Gerard Cauvin was ambitious for his sons, especially the bright and studious John. They all attended the school of Capettes, the best in the city, which was named after the hooded cloaks the boys wore. John did notably well, and clearly had the potential of going far in life. He was a serious and conscientious student, but he was also very sociable and had a number of friends with whom he maintained contact for many years. However education was not cheap, and in order to finance it Gerard used his influence with the bishop and cathedral chapter to secure for his sons ecclesiastical offices from which they would receive an income: at the age of twelve John was given the chaplaincy of the La Gésine, an altar in the cathedral for which he received three measures of corn and the wheat of twenty fields. The income paid both

Dr.L.H.Lee

for John's education and a priest to fulfil his duties! This meant that Calvin had become a clerk on the lowest rung of the ecclesiastical ladder and was able to wear the tonsure, the special haircut of the clergy that left the crown of the head bare. A few years later he was given the curacy of the church of St Martin de Martheville which was later exchanged for another church in Pont-l'Evêque. These arrangements were common practice in the Church at the time and were among the many abuses that some wanted to reform. However, for Calvin it meant that his schooling was paid for and he would be able to study at university.

University in Paris

Gerard Cauvin's intention was that all his sons should become priests. As a conventionally devout man he would have believed such a vocation a good thing in itself, but as an ambitious father he also would have seen the priesthood as offering good career prospects for his boys. So, when John was eleven he was sent off to university in Paris in the company of three of his school friends from Noyon and their tutor. Coming from a relatively small city to a large city such as Paris must have been a remarkable experience for a young teenager. Gerard arranged for his son to lodge with his uncle Richard, a blacksmith who lived close to the church of Saint-Germain l'Auxerrois near the university.

The Paris that Calvin came to as a student was nothing like the Paris we know today. We are familiar with the wide boulevards, but Calvin's Paris was a large medieval city of densely packed buildings and narrow crooked streets. At its heart was the Cathedral of Notre Dame that Calvin would have seen often. Then, as now, the university was located on the left bank of the River Seine. Today it is popularly known as

Top: *The ruins of the Abbey of Ourskamp which Calvin visited as a child with his mother*
Left: *The interior of Noyon Cathedral*

Above: *The Cathedral of Notre Dame in Paris*

the Sorbonne, but when Calvin was a student the Sorbonne was strictly the theological faculty for which the university was famous. Presided over by the austere Noel Beda, the Sorbonne was the guardian of orthodoxy and would become a bitter opponent of the new theological thinking spreading out from Germany.

Initially Calvin enrolled in a course that would prepare him for an arts degree allowing him then to study for a degree in theology, law or medicine. This preparatory course was primarily one in Latin grammar intended to bring the students up to the necessary standard. The University of Paris was divided into a number of colleges and Calvin's was the Collège de la Marche. The teaching of Latin in the college to the first year students was not of a high standard, and matters came to a head about the time Calvin arrived which turned out to his advantage. One of the college's most distinguished teachers, Mathurin Cordier, volunteered to teach the first year students in order to try to sort things out. He did away with the tedious methods that had been used and aimed instead to inspire his students and put an emphasis on conversation and elegance of style. In addition, he was personally very kind to students; Calvin never forgot Cordier's teaching, and thirty years later dedicated his commentary on 1 Thessalonians to him recalling that, 'God's goodness gave you to me for a little while as preceptor, to teach me the true way to learn so that I might continue with greater profit.' Cordier's influence was instrumental in instilling in Calvin a love for

Photo by André Leroux

languages that would bear fruit in his study of the Bible. It was perhaps to Cordier that Calvin owed his ability to write in the excellent Latin and French that he did. Cordier came to Geneva thirty years later at Calvin's invitation to teach in the new academy there. In addition to Latin Calvin also studied logic, especially Aristotle, and some mathematics.

After a year, Calvin was considered to have the capability of commencing the arts course, and so he transferred to the Collège de Montaigu. This was one of the oldest colleges in the university with an illustrious past and many famous alumni. Erasmus, the great Dutch theologian, had spent some time here, and after Calvin left Ignatius Loyola, founder of the Jesuits, arrived. Unfortunately, by Calvin's time the college had declined, and it was then infamous for its filth, bad food, vermin, damp and the strict discipline with which the students were to live. The writer Rabelais, a former student, called the lice on its walls: 'the short-winged hawks of Montaigu', and Erasmus remembered the many rotten eggs he had eaten there. Its director was a man named Tempete whom the students nick-named 'The Tempest' for his tyrannical and brutal regime. He often whipped students who misbehaved.

College life was rigorous. The day began at 4.00 am, although Calvin may have been able to start later as he lived with his uncle. After Mass there was breakfast and then lectures until 11.00 and a break for lunch. Then followed a session when the students were questioned, others classes, a rest period, vespers, supper, and more classes or question sessions before bed. On two afternoons each week

Dr.L.H.Lee

Top: *The Church of Saint-Germain l'Auxerrois. The ringing of its 'Marie' bell on St Bartholomew's Day 1572 was the signal to begin the massacre of Protestants in Paris*
Left: *The Sorbonne today*

Right: The Bibliotheque St Geneviève on the site of the Collège de la Marche

the students were allowed to take some recreation. However, as much as the university authorities would have liked the students to behave in an orderly way, they didn't. The street between Montaigu and the Collège du Sainte-Barbe was the scene of many student fights as well as the home of much low life. It was also notoriously filthy with much of the sewage from the colleges running into it.

However, Calvin devoted himself to his studies and established a reputation as a brilliant student. When he completed his grammatical studies he proceeded to the philosophy course in which, as well as being grounded in medieval Roman Catholic theology, he was trained in rigorous logical analysis and

The Renaissance and Humanism

Calvin was educated in an intellectual and cultural environment known as the Renaissance. The Renaissance was a cultural movement in Europe from the 14th to the 17th centuries. The peak of its influence was in the 16th century around the time of the Reformation. It had many facets, among which was a rediscovery of classical antiquity and particularly classical literature and philosophy. Scholars sought to renew the church and wider culture by engaging the classical heritage of Europe. Their slogan was *ad fontes*, Latin for 'to the sources'. Another name for this movement is Humanism, not in the sense of secular humanism today, but rather in the sense of a rediscovery of what it means to be human as understood by classical authors. As well as returning to classical writings, scholars also returned to the original text of the Bible. Like many humanist scholars of his day Calvin learned Hebrew and Greek in order to study the Bible in the original languages. A pioneer in this was the Dutch scholar Erasmus who exercised immense intellectual influence. However his concern was not only academic; he sought to reform the corrupt church by reemphasising the Bible. Erasmus fell far short of the doctrinal reforms that Luther, Calvin and the other Reformers sought, and came to oppose them. Nevertheless the Renaissance prepared the way for the Reformation.

Left: A café on the Left Bank of Paris in the area where Calvin studied and lived

Below: The Pantheon on the site of the Collège Montaigu

argumentation. By the end of 1527 or early 1528 be had completed the course and received his Master of Arts. While Calvin had no trouble intellectually with his studies, his severe self-discipline seems to have taken a physical toll. He complained of headaches and stomach pains. Even as a young man he was not physically robust and was, as he would always be, both thin and gaunt.

During his time in Paris, Calvin made a large group of friends. He always valued friendship and it is evident that he had a capacity for making friends to whom he remained loyal and who remained loyal to him. Already in Paris he had his friends from Noyon as well as his distant cousin Pierre Robert, later known as Oliévtan, who translated the Bible into French and became an evangelist in the French Alps. Perhaps his closest friend was Nicolas Cop, the son of Guillaume Cop, the royal physician and a member of the medical faculty. Cop senior was a friend of Erasmus and sympathetic to the new learning the Dutchman advocated. Calvin often visited the Cop home and probably participated in conversations that opened his eyes to many of the new ideas that were circulating in the academic

Photo by David Monniaux © 2007

world. Nicolas was four years older than Calvin and would become, at a relatively young age, the rector of the university. His younger brother Michel was also close to Calvin and later became a Reformed pastor in Geneva. But while Calvin's warm and deep friendships suggest an attractive and winsome character, there was another side to Calvin mentioned by some early biographers, even those sympathetic to him. He seems to have been a little censorious of the conduct of others, and apparently was known by some fellow students as 'the accusative case'. His friend and Geneva colleague, Theodore Beza, approvingly says that as a student Calvin used to censor the vices of other students, which would not have made him a popular student on campus.

Further study in Orléans and Bourges

As John was finishing his first degree in Paris, his father changed his mind with regard to his son's future. Instead of becoming a priest, Gerard decided that John should become a lawyer, and therefore from the study of theology Calvin now studied law. Exactly why Gerard made this change we are not sure. Part of the problem may have been that Gerard had fallen out with the bishop and chapter in Noyon. Apparently he had been asked to produce some accounts which he refused to submit for some reason. Perhaps he had mishandled money or was simply annoyed or disillusioned with the church. On the other hand, his decision may have been a cool calculation that a career in the church was not as good as it once had been. Calvin himself thought this was the explanation. Whatever the exact

Top right: *An old view of the university of Paris*
Bottom right: *The Salle des Thèses—the oldest remaining part of Orléans University*

Photo by Patrick Giraud

reason, Gerard told John that he should shift to a law course and John complied.

Orléans was a very different university from Paris. It was a far more relaxed place, and the students were known for their enjoyment of sailing and tennis. There were around forty tennis courts in the city, but it is doubtful if the serious and studious Calvin frequented them. In Orléans the spirit of the Renaissance was dominant and the new humanistic learning was more welcome. In the law faculty civil law was more prominent than canon or ecclesiastical law. Here there were brilliant teachers such as Pierre de l'Estoile.

As he had done in Paris, Calvin threw himself into his studies. He was remembered for eating a light supper, studying until midnight, then waking early the next morning to review all that he had studied the night before. Even so, Calvin had time for his friends. Jean and Claude Hangest, boyhood friends from Noyon, were there, as was Pierre Robert and Nicolas de Chemin with whom he had lodged for a time in Paris. Calvin wrote to the latter as 'my friend, dearer than my life.' He made new friends as well, most notably Francois Daniel who was from Orléans and in whose family home Calvin spent many hours. The earliest

Top: *Orléans today*
Left: *The interior of Salle des Theses where Calvin may have worked*

letters we have by Calvin were written to these friends. One of them was also one of his teachers.

Melchior Wolmar was fourteen years older than Calvin; he taught Greek and it was under his tutelage that Calvin mastered the language that would enable him later to become such a brilliant exegete of the New Testament. Later Calvin dedicated his commentary on 2 Corinthians to Wolmar. But perhaps Wolmar had an even greater influence on Calvin. He was committed to the evangelical faith and may have won Calvin to it; it is almost certain that by this time Calvin was moving away from Roman Catholicism to evangelicalism and Wolmar's influence may have been instrumental.

After a year in Orléans , Calvin decided to pursue his legal studies in Bourges. The reason seems to have been a desire to sit under the teaching of the celebrated jurist Andreas Alciati who was drawing many students to Bourges. His approach was to go back to the original texts and to interpret them grammatically within their historical and cultural contexts, much as Erasmus and others were doing with the Bible. Calvin spent eighteen months in Bourges, continuing his Greek studies with Wolmar who had been recruited to the university. It was while studying with Wolmar that Calvin met a twelve year old student named Theodore de Beze (Beza). Like Calvin, Beza was an able student and later worked with him in Geneva and succeeded him as the chief pastor there. There is a tradition that during this time Calvin preached in villages near Bourges.

Calvin returned to Paris in 1531, possibly during the university vacation, and while there he heard that his father had been taken ill. John returned to his boyhood home where his father died about twelve days later. Gerard's quarrel with the

Photo by Renaud Mavré

Above: *Bourges Cathedral*

church had not been settled, and his sons had to work hard to persuade the authorities to allow his body to be buried in consecrated ground. After the funeral, Calvin spent about a month in Noyon sorting out his father's affairs with his brother Charles. Gerard's death meant that John no longer had to take his wishes into account for his future life. Increasingly, Calvin was less inclined to law and more to the life of a scholar.

Return to Paris

In the early 1530s Calvin moved back to Paris. This was an exciting time to be in the city for a thoughtful young man like Calvin since it was a time of intellectual ferment as new ideas were being hotly debated. King Francis I had established what became known as Collège de France in 1530 with the appointment of a number of Royal Lecturers. These men promoted the new learning pioneered by Erasmus and others. Taking a room in Collège de Fortet near Collège du Montaigu, Calvin devoted himself to humanistic studies, especially Greek, Latin and Hebrew. He studied Greek under Pierre Danes and Hebrew under Francois Vatable, both Royal Lecturers. Making life in Paris all the more enjoyable were many of his friends as well as his brother Antoine. Once again Calvin enjoyed the generous hospitality and stimulating conversation of the Cop home.

But life wasn't easy. Money was a problem since his brother Charles did not manage the family affairs well in Noyon and Calvin seems to have had to borrow from friends. And now Charles himself was also in trouble with the cathedral chapter in Noyon! He had been accused of heresy of some kind. Was he picking up some Protestant ideas and if so was his brother John at least partly responsible? We do not know. But Charles was never reconciled to the church by the time of his death, and the Cauvin or Calvin name has never been in favour in Noyon since.

Towards the end of 1531 Calvin completed his *Commentary on Seneca's* De Clementia (On Clemency). It was his first book and was published

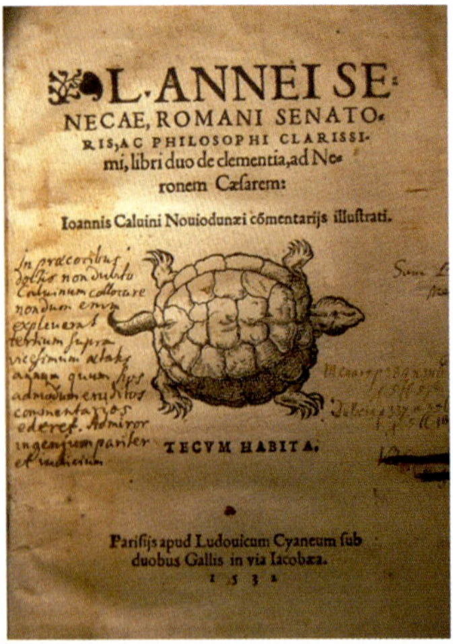
L. ANNEI SENECAE, ROMANI SENATORIS, AC PHILOSOPHI CLARISSIMI, libri duo de clementia, ad Neronem Cæsarem:

Ioannis Caluini Nouiodunæi cõmentarijs illuſtrati.

TECVM HABITA.

Pariſijs apud Ludouicum Cyaneum ſub duobus Gallis in via Iacobæa.

1532

Left: *The title page to Calvin's first book*
Opposite top: *The chapter room in Noyon Cathedral*

in April of the following year and established his reputation as a promising scholar of the first rank. It took him eight months of hard work and was a commentary on a book by the Roman stoic philosopher Seneca, who was a contemporary of the apostle Paul. The catalyst may have been the earlier publication of Erasmus' edition of Seneca's works. Printed at his own expense, Calvin dedicated the book to his childhood friend Claude de Hangest who was now the abbot of Sainte-Éloi in Noyon. The bulk of the book consisted of historical, exegetical, and explanatory comments on Seneca's treatise on clemency. Calvin's annotations revealed a maturity of judgment and acquaintance with ancient writers that was remarkable for a young scholar. The strong moral and ethical tone of Seneca's writing seems to have attracted him, although he critiqued his stoic philosophy. The book was also written in the excellent Latin that would later characterize Calvin's writing. However, it was hardly a bestseller and he had to beg friends to buy copies and even sent one to Erasmus.

It is not easy to keep track of Calvin in the early 1530s. His correspondence reveals that he went back to Orléans for a time where he was elected as the dean of students from his home region of Picardy. Universities at the time were organized into regional 'nations' for administrative purposes. Calvin was reasonably popular, although some students must have had second thoughts when he gave the money collected for his election party to the university library! In August 1533 Calvin was back again in Noyon for a meeting of the cathedral chapter and then back in Paris. For Calvin, a life of quiet scholarship looked like it beckoned, but within a short time things took a very different turn.

NOYON

Key to places
1 Cathedral
2 Musée Calvin
3 Port Corbault
4 Renaissance Library
5 Hotel de Ville

TRAVEL INFORMATION

Noyon

Noyon is a pleasant French provincial city about 90 km northwest of Paris. It is one of three Picardy cathedral cities, the others being Laon and Soissons. Together they are worth a day or two visiting in their own right or if travelling between Paris and Calais. There is also a vast former royal place in nearby Compiègne. Noyon has been the seat of a bishopric since 531. In 768 Charlemagne was crowned here as king of Nuestria and in 987 Hugh Capet was crowned king of France. During the First World War the town, including Calvin's birthplace, was largely destroyed and had to be rebuilt. The cathedral with its library is the main attraction. The former bishop's palace now houses the Musée du Noyonnais which among other things displays the cathedral's treasures. Calvin's reconstructed birthplace is now the Musée Calvin at 6, place Aristade Briand. There are a number of items on display relating to Calvin and the Reformation in France. www.ville-noyon.fr or www.noyon-tourisme.com.

Below:
Hotel de Ville in Noyon

Paris

—see travel information at the end of the next chapter.

Orléans

Located about 100 km southwest of Paris, Orléans is situated at the northern edge of the Loire with its many magnificent chateaux. The city is famous for its association with Joan of Arc. As well as a museum devoted to her there are a number of others including the Musée des Beaux Arts next to the Cathedral. While Orléans is an interesting city to visit there are no sites directly related to Calvin. There is however an interesting circular Reformed Church or Temple opened in 1839 at Cloitre Saint Pierre Emport in the centre of the city.
Not far from Orléans is the cathedral city of Chartres.
www.tourisme-Orleans .com.

Bourges

Bourges is smaller than Orléans and lies about 90km further south. It has a spectacular cathedral as well as a number of older mansions and half-timbered houses that give some impression of the city that Calvin knew. While there are no sites with direct Calvin links there is a Reformed church at 3 rue Vielle-Saint-Ambroix , just north of the city centre.
www.ville-bourges.fr

2 'A sudden conversion'

Calvin's life was turned around when he was suddenly converted. His new evangelical faith meant that he became a fugitive and an exile, but in the process he discovered his life's calling to be a pastor and preacher of God's word

When Calvin arrived back in Paris in 1533 after his studies in Orlèans and Bourges, he found that the intellectual and religious climate was very different from when he had been a student there before. In part this was due to the attitude of the king, Francis I, who encouraged the new learning associated with Erasmus and the French scholar Jacques Lefèvre. The Sorbonne was still fiercely opposed to them, but when they criticized the king's sister, Beda and several colleagues were expelled. During Lent that year, Gérard Rousel, another evangelical sympathizer and a friend of Calvin, delivered a series of sermons that aroused the opposition of the faculty. However, most significant was the election of Calvin's friend Nicolas Cop as rector of the university. He was known as a reformist or evangelical and used his rectoral address to promote the new teaching. Speaking in the Church of the Mathurins, he took his text from Matthew 5:3, 'Blessed are the poor in spirit'; Cop spoke about the grace of God in an evangelical way that echoed his reading of Erasmus and Luther. It was rumoured then, and now, that Calvin may have had a hand in writing the address.

The religious authorities were angry at what Cop said. They accused him of heresy and demanded that something be done. Nothing much happened until about a month later in November when he was warned of his impending arrest. Cop was leading a university procession, and at a convenient moment he slipped down a side street and escaped. He

Facing Page: A young John Calvin
© MHR

Right: Church of the Mathurins in Paris

fled from Paris to Basel. The police then went to arrest Calvin, but he too was warned and escaped from his room at the Collège de Fortet through a rear window. For the next few years Calvin would be a fugitive.

Conversion

At some point during this period Calvin experienced conversion. There is debate among students of Calvin about this, but it probably happened at some point between 1529 and 1531 when he was studying law in Orlèans and Bourges, although some scholars place it a few years later. Exactly how it happened we do not know, although Calvin was open to the new learning and moved in circles sympathetic to evangelical theology. Some years later in 1557 he wrote of his conversion in his preface to the *Commentary on the Psalms*. The autobiographical nature of some of the psalms seems to have moved him to write of his own experience of God working in his life. He wrote of his humble origins compared with David and of how his father had directed him to change his studies to law. Though he had dutifully obeyed, he came to see subsequently that 'God finally made me turn about in another direction by his secret providence.' This new direction began with his conversion. He writes of how he was 'obstinately addicted to the superstitions of the papacy' and in a 'deep slough' that it was only 'by a sudden conversion' that God 'subdued me and reduced my heart to docility.'

Providentially God had used Calvin's circumstances and people like his cousin Oliévtan and his friend and teacher Wolmar, but the change was a supernatural work of God in Calvin's heart. From now on, much as he loved his study of classical literature and law, Calvin now had something that demanded even greater devotion. While, as a naturally shy person, he wanted to devote himself to study and 'loved quiet and tranquility', he found to his astonishment that wherever he went he was sought out for instruction in the faith.

Above: *The plaque indicating Calvin's connection with the College*

Left: *The site of the Collège de Fortet on rue Valette*

Through many dangers

By 1533 Calvin had to leave Paris in the aftermath of Nicolas Cop's address because he was now a Protestant or evangelical. Heading north, Calvin made his way to Noyon where he stayed for a few weeks until it was safe to return to Paris. When he did return, he met with Margaret, the king's sister, who continued to intercede with her brother for the reformists. Nevertheless Calvin felt it wiser to leave Paris and he stayed at Claix near Angoulême with another friend from his student days, Louis du Tillet who was a parish priest. Calvin may have spent four or five months in

Photo by Heurtelions

Above: *'Calvin's tower' in the courtyard of the building on the site of the Collège de Fortet on rue Valette*

Humanism

The leading humanist scholar in France was Jacques Lefèvre. In 1512 he had published a Latin translation and commentary on Paul's epistles in which he wrote of the grace of God. Not surprisingly he was not content for the New Testament to be only a matter of academic study and he began translating it into French so that common people could read the Bible for themselves. Lefèvre worked closely with Briçonnet, the bishop of Meaux, not far from Paris. Briçonnet himself began to preach from the Bible and made Meaux

Jacques Lefèvre

a centre for church reform and renewal. It has been suggested that the king's sister, Margaret d'Angoulème, had been converted to the evangelical faith though him. However, as the new ideas spread, so did opposition to them. The centre of the opposition was the Sorbonne whose theologians were able to have Lefèvre put out of the university and his writings condemned. The New Testament that he had translated was publicly burnt. Lefevre fled, but Briçonnet repudiated his earlier teaching. In different cities ordinary men and women were charged with heresy and burned at the stake. Some spoke movingly of their faith as they prepared to die. Nevertheless the reform movement continued to grow in France. Luther's writings were being translated into French and printed secretly, and people continued to meet to discuss the new ideas.

Above: *Angoulême*

Claix where he seems to have taken the opportunity to use du Tillet's extensive library, and he may have begun to write there *The Institutes of the Christian Religion*, the book for which he is best known and that he would revise over many years. Whilst here, Calvin taught Tillett Greek and met with a number of evangelical sympathizers in the area.

In April 1534 Calvin travelled south to Nérac, the capital of the small kingdom of Navarre. Margaret had become Queen of Navarre and made it a haven for reformists and evangelicals. The

Martin Luther

Calvin always acknowledged his debt to Martin Luther. Although Luther disagreed with him on the nature of the Lord's Supper, Calvin would never hear a bad word against him. When he was a student in Paris, Luther's teaching about the gospel was beginning to infiltrate France. The ground had been prepared in France by scholars like Erasmus and Lefévre, but it was Luther who became the leader of the Reformation movement. Born in Eisleben in 1483 in what is today Germany, Luther became a monk and a professor of theology at the University of Wittenburg. After an immense spiritual struggle he came to see from his study of Paul's Letter to the Romans that God justifies sinners through faith alone in Jesus Christ and not in any measure on the basis of their good works. This discovery ran counter to

Martin Luther

the teaching and practice of the Roman Catholic Church with the authorities of which Luther increasingly came into conflict. Famously he nailed 95 Theses to the door of the castle church in Wittenburg on 31 October 1517 as a challenge for a debate. Later he had to defend himself before various church assemblies convened to deal with the new 'heresy'. Back in Wittenburg Luther continued to advance reform by preaching, lecturing, writing and organizing. His teaching spread throughout Europe, helped by the recently invented printing press which meant that his writings were cheaply and easily available in many places. No doubt Calvin read some of them secretly as a student. Luther died in 1546. The churches most directly influenced by him eventually became known as Lutheran and were strongest in northern Germany and Scandinavia. On various points they differed from the Reformed churches that were more influenced by Calvin, but on the central truth of the gospel of God's grace in Christ they agreed.

Photo by Jean-Baptiste Malaubie

elderly Lefévre had moved there to spend his last years and Calvin visited him. Tradition relates that during this time, Calvin preached in different places, but it is more likely that he kept himself to his studies and private meetings. Years later du Tillet, who had returned to Roman Catholicism, said that when with him Calvin had not dared to publicly express his views.

For Calvin, the time had come to sever his links with the church. He went back to Noyon for the last time in May 1534 to resign his chaplaincy and benefices from which he received an income. He was now 25 years of age which was the traditional age when a cleric like Calvin would proceed to the priesthood, but he was turning his back on that life and trusting God for the future. Whatever career he might have had in the church was now closed to him. However, ending his church career was not without its problems. While Calvin was in Noyon he was imprisoned on two occasions, though the circumstances are mysterious. He was arrested the first time after a riot in a church on 26 May and imprisoned for just over a week in La Porte Corbaut which can still be seen. Two days after his release, he was rearrested and may have spent several weeks in prison. Whether the arrests were related to the reform movement is not clear. Later some of Calvin's critics used this episode to suggest that he had been arrested for some kind of impropriety, but there is no evidence for this.

Above right: *La Porte Corbaut in Noyon where Calvin was imprisoned*

Bottom right: *'The Candlestick' shows the unity of Protestantism. Calvin is to its right and Luther to its left. 17th century*

Photo by jibi44

***Above:** The palace of Margaret of Navarre at Nérac*

Fugitive

After his release, Calvin left Noyon, and for the next few years he was moving from place to place with his life often in danger. He later wrote, 'God so led me about through different turnings and changes, that he never permitted me to rest in any place …' He headed for Paris where for several weeks he met secretly with friends and evangelical sympathizers. Meetings were always in danger of being detected and broken up, but Calvin was certain that his was God's cause and that whatever happened to him, God would prevail. Apparently he would end his addresses with the words of Paul from Romans chapter 8, 'If God be for us, who can be against us?'

Friends were now urging him to leave Paris, so he headed west to Angoulême and Poitiers. There is evidence that he preached in different places, although it is doubtful if this was too public. It seems that he celebrated the Lord's Supper in a cave outside Poitiers. Unlike the Roman Mass, Calvin's service was simple and Bible based. Here in Poitiers he began to pioneer a new understanding of congregational worship that he would develop later in Geneva and Strasbourg. Here also, a number of men who later became eminent Reformed pastors were influenced by Calvin though conversations and discussions. He was beginning to exercise the pastoral and evangelistic ministry that would become his life's calling.

A second book

At some point, Calvin returned to Orléans where he spent enough time to complete his second book *Psychpannychia* or *On soul sleep*. This was a very different book from his first. The doctrine of soul sleep taught that on death the soul of a Christian goes to sleep until the return of Christ and the resurrection of the dead. The doctrine was popular among

***Above:** Poitiers today*

Anabaptists who were gaining influence, and would become a life-long concern for Calvin. On this issue Calvin answered the false teaching from the Bible which he summed up in these words: 'The souls of the saints, who die in the faith of Christ, do not sleep, but live in Christ.' Why he chose this subject is not clear; perhaps it was a significant issue for the people among whom he was ministering. Of more significance was the preface to the book; in this he wrote of being called to be a teacher of Christian doctrine: 'If in such need I am silent or dissimulate, I do not see why I should not be called a betrayer of the truth.' During this time he also wrote two prefaces to French translations of the Bible by his cousin Oliévtan.

Calvin may have returned to Paris in the autumn of 1534, but if he did, he soon had to flee again. On 18 October placards appeared all over Paris, as well in some other French cities, protesting against the church and in particular the Mass which was described as 'a great, horrible and unendurable abuse.' One was even posted on the king's bedroom door! Francis was livid and the incident turned him finally against the reform movement. Two hundred people were arrested and twenty were executed. By the end of January an edict against Lutherans was issued. By that time Calvin had left the city, and with his friend Louis du Tillet and two servants he made his way eastwards to Strasbourg, adopting the name Martianus Lacanius to hide his identity. Along the way he and du Tillet must often have feared recognition and arrest. In fact all that happened was that one of the servants robbed them of their money and one of their horses and they had to borrow money from the other servant

to complete their journey. Throughout all this, Calvin was suffering from the severe headaches and stomach pains he would endure through most of his life.

Exile

The party made their way to Strasbourg which was the home of Martin Bucer and who no doubt would have welcomed them; however, for some reason they stayed there only for a short time and continued until they reached Basel where they arrived early in 1535. Basel was a well-known centre of learning and printing and was one of the centres of reform in Switzerland; for Calvin it had the added attraction of being the refuge for his friend Nicolas Cop. Calvin and du Tillet found lodging with a Madame Catherine Klein where they stayed for a year.

Back in Paris, however, many suffered for their evangelical beliefs. Among them, Etienne de la Forge in whose house Calvin had lodged and who had been a great encourager. He was executed in a most horrific fashion as were many others.

Top: *Strasbourg where Calvin first found refuge and where years later he would spend some of the happiest years of his life*

Right: *Martin Bucer the principal reformer in Strasbourg and a good friend of Calvin who later would teach at Cambridge in England*

Photo by Wladyslaw Sojka

Above: *The cathedral in Basel. Calvin and du Tillet first arrived in the city in 1535*

Three of Margaret's evangelical chaplains were arrested. She pleaded with her brother the king for the evangelicals, but he was deaf to her pleas. He did, however, release her three chaplains into the care of a monastery. There two of them recanted, but the third, Courauld, escaped and fled to Basel where he brought news to Calvin of what was happening in France.

While in Basel, Calvin began or perhaps completed writing the first edition of the book for which he would become most well-known: *The Institutes of the Christian Religion*. It was printed in February 1536 and was available in the bookstalls in March. Calvin would live with the *Institutes* for the rest of his life, regularly revising and expanding it. In its final version in 1559 it had grown some six times in size and had become a complete guide to the Christian faith.

By the time the *Institutes* was published in March 1536, Calvin and du Tillet had left Basel. Calvin assumed a new name, Charles d'Espeville, which literally means 'city of hope', perhaps expressing his conviction that in God he would be vindicated in heaven if not on earth. The two men headed across the Alps to Ferrara in northern Italy. Ferrara was the home of Renée of France, a daughter of Louis XII and cousin of Francis and Margaret, who was unhappily married to Hercules, the Duke of Ferrara. The Duke was the son of the infamous Lucrezia Borgia and the grandson of a pope! Previously Renée had been engaged to Henry VIII, but nothing came of it which, considering Henry's record, was perhaps fortunate for her.

The Duke's court was magnificent and centred on his enormous brick castle that can still be seen in Ferrara. Renée welcomed her compatriots and fellow evangelicals and conversed often with them during their brief stay. Her secretary was another Frenchman, Clément Marot, who may have told her about Calvin and who later joined Calvin in Geneva where he wrote poetry and set many of the psalms to metrical verse. It is possible that Renée wanted Calvin to stay in her service, but he declined. He did not like Italy and churlishly commented, 'I only went to Italy that I might have the pleasure of leaving it.' More serious was the increasing hostility of Hercules to evangelical religion and his suspicions of many of his wife's visitors.

So, after a month, Calvin and du Tillet left Ferrara and headed back to France through Switzerland. There is a tradition that Calvin preached in some of the villages on the way, but that is unlikely considering the hostility of the political and religious authorities. After Calvin's departure, Renée suffered much for her faith and at one point was imprisoned and had her children taken from her to be raised as Roman Catholics. After her husband's death she returned to France where she supported the Protestant cause. Until the end of his life Calvin continued to write to Renée to encourage her in her faith. His last letter was dictated to her in order to assure her of the honour in which he and other French evangelicals held her.

Renée of France, cousin of the French king, fervent evangelical and life-long friend of Calvin

Calvin and du Tillet headed for Basel and then to Paris which was safer for evangelicals again because of an amnesty decreed by the king. There Calvin met his sister Marie and brother Antoine, and together they agreed to move as a family to Strasbourg. Charles had died and another sister was a devout Catholic. Before he died Charles was accused of heresy and refused the sacrament. Had he too become an evangelical? We do not know, but now in 1536 most of the children of Gérard Cauvin were identified with the evangelical cause and sought refuge in a city congenial to their faith. Unfortunately the direct route to Strasbourg was blocked by troop movements, and so Calvin decided to take a longer route that would lead him through the small city of Geneva. Little did he know that his name would become linked with this city with consequences that are still with us.

Above: *The Swiss Alps which Calvin would have had to cross on his way to Italy*

Photo by Tommaso.Gavioli

Left: *Ancient and modern: A fly past over the Ducal castle at Ferrara where Renée lived as wife of the Duke*

TRAVEL INFORMATION

Paris

Paris is one of the world's great cities with a vast array of things to see and do. Calvin spent much of his time on what is today called the Left Bank in the area around the **Sorbonne**, the original University of Paris. Today as then the neighbourhood is known as the Latin Quarter. It is a fascinating area to explore on foot with numerous museums, churches, cafes and sites such as the **Panthéon**. None of the buildings from Calvin's time remain except churches such as **St Germain-des Pres** next to the **Metro station** that bears its name on Boulevard Saint-Germain. The main building of the

PARIS

1 The Sorbonne
2 The Panthéon
3 The church of St Germain-des-Pres
4 Rue Valette (sight of the Collège Fortet)
5 Biblioteque Saint-Genevieve
6 Palais du Luxembourg
7 The Cathedral of Notre Dame
8 The Louvre Museum
9 The Oratoire du Louvre
10 The monument to Gaspard de Coligny
11 Place des Vosges

Photo by Jibi44

Top:
Sacre-Coeur in Paris
Below: *Nérac today*

Sorbonne is on rue Victor Cousin. The street to the north of the Panthéon is **rue Valette** where at number 21 is a building on the site of the **Collége de Fortet** where Calvin lived for some of his time in Paris. There is a plaque bearing Calvin's portrait and a biographical note. On the corner of rue Valette and the place du Panthéon is the **Biblioteque Saint-Geneviève** on the site of the Collège Montaigu that Calvin attended. On the upper wall are inscribed the names of famous French writers including that of Calvin. To the west of the Pantheon is the **Palais du Luxembourg** surrounded by its beautiful gardens. Built in the 1620s, the palace was designed by the famous French Protestant architect Salomon de Brosse for Marie de Medici, the widow of Henri IV.

The **Cathedral of Notre Dame** is located on the Ile de Cite in the Seine. On the other side of the river is the famous **Louvre Museum**. Across the street at its northeast corner on the rue de Rivoli is the **L'Oratoire de Louvre**, the main Reformed Church in Paris. It was built in 1621 and given by Napoleon to the Reformed Church in 1802. The interior is a classical Protestant auditorium. On the street opposite the Louvre is a monument dedicated to the memory of **Admiral Gaspard de Coligny**, a friend of Calvin and the aristocratic leader of French Protestants in the mid-16th century. He was killed in the St Bartholomew's Day Massacre in 1572 (see page 121). Nearby is a street that bears his name. Further east is the splendid and tranquil **Place des Vosges** that was built by Henri IV and designed by Salomon de Brosse. The houses reveal the prosperity and taste of the original 16th century residents, a number of which were well-known Protestants.

The sites described here are within reasonably easy walking distance of each other. Walking about Paris is one of its delights. The Paris Metro system is easy to use and because of the short distances between stations there is usually one relatively near to most sites.

For more information on Protestant Paris see www.erf-rp.org where there is a description of Protestant sites in Paris.

For more general information see www.parisinfo.com.

Strasbourg

—see chapter 4

Nérac

Nérac is a small town in Lot-et-Garonne in the south-west of France about half way between Bordeaux

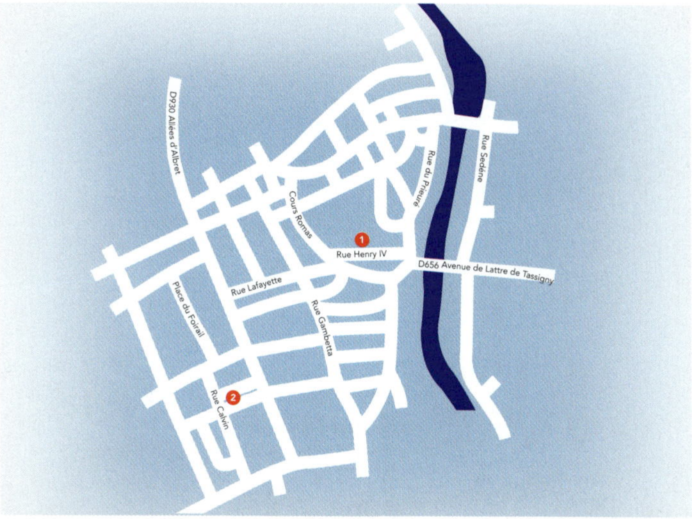

NERAC

1 Château de Nérac (Castle) **2** Protestant Temple

to the northwest and Montauban to the south-east. Its main attraction is the remaining wing of the **Castle** where Calvin stayed when he went to see Lefevre there. There are a number of interesting buildings, some of them medieval, on either side of the Baise River that give an impression of what the town was like in Calvin's time. The **Protestant Temple** at 35, allées d'Albret was built in 1858 and is a replica of the temple in La Rochelle destroyed at the Revocation of the Edict of Nantes. Further south is the town of Orthez that Jeanne d'Albret, the Protestant mother of Henri IV, made the capital the kingdom of Navarre. The **Musée Jeanne d'Albret** at 37 rue Bourg Vieux, is devoted to the history of Protestantism in the Bearn region. There is a fine **Protestant temple** at 20 rue General Foy.

For more information see www.useejeanned'albret.com.

Ferrara

The lovely city of Ferrara, situated on the plain between Venice and Bologna, is dominated by the Castello Estense that Calvin visited. The enormous castle is built, like much of the city, with brick and surrounded by a moat. It is open to visitors. The d'Este family were great patrons of the arts and the city benefited as a result. There are a number of other museums, palaces and churches well worth visiting. To commemorate the reformer's visit the city authorities a named a street Via Giovanni Calvino. For more information see www.artecultura.fe.it.

Above: *The Palais du Luxembourg in Paris*

Photo by Wouter Hagens

3 Geneva—the first time

By an unpredicted turn of events Calvin ended up devoting his life to the people of the small city state of Geneva. However, his first ministry here he later referred to as 'torture'. Nevertheless there were lessons to be learned and a foundation was laid for future work

Calvin intended to spend only a night in Geneva on his way to Strasbourg, but he had not reckoned on William Farel. When Farel was told that Calvin was in the city he went straight to the house where he was staying and told him in no uncertain terms that it was his duty to stay. This is Calvin's account of what happened that night.

> 'William Farel forced me to stay in Geneva not so much by advice or urging as by command, which had the power of God's hand laid violently upon me from heaven. … Farel, who was working with incredible zeal to promote the gospel, bent all his efforts to keep me in the city. And when he realized that I was determined to study in privacy in some obscure place, and saw that he gained nothing by entreaty, he descended to cursing, and said that God would surely curse my peace if I held back from giving help at a time of such great need. Terrified by his words, and conscious of my open timidity and cowardice, I gave up my journey and attempted to apply whatever gift I had in defence of my faith.'

Calvin had some affairs to attend to in Basel, but within a few weeks he was back in Geneva where together with Farel and Courauld he would work for reformation.

***Facing page:** The Cathedral of St Pierre in Geneva*

***Right:** Geneva today—the Jet d'Eau*

Photo by Jiji

Facing page: An old drawing of Geneva

Left: Geneva from the lake

Below: Antoine Froment preaching the Reformation in Geneva. 19th century painting

William Farel was a stocky, well-built man with a red beard and a tempestuous and forceful personality. Erasmus once said of him: 'Never in my life have I seen so bold a man.' He had been working in Geneva for four years to promote the evangelical faith. Geneva was not in fact part of Switzerland, but an independent city republic, and had only recently broken free from the control of the Duke of Savoy. In 1528, under political pressure from the powerful canton of Berne, it declared for the Reformation and expelled the Prince-Bishop of the city. Nevertheless the religious situation in the city remained unsettled. Farel had been preaching with the support of the authorities in Bern in the French-speaking areas under its control. Seeing an opportunity in Geneva, he arrived in 1532 and began meeting with evangelical sympathizers and preaching

© MHR

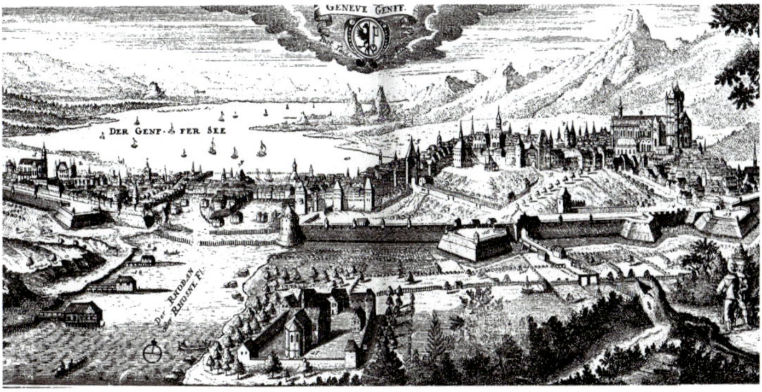

in the open air. The priests in the city reacted angrily and attacked Farel who was forced to flee. He returned the next year accompanied by Antoine Froment and Pierre Viret. As a result of their preaching and public disputations, the number of evangelicals grew significantly so that, on 27 August 1535, Roman Catholicism was finally repudiated and the Reformation

William Farel (1489–1565)

Farel played an important role in the reformation not only of Geneva, but of several other cities as well. He was born in Gap in south-eastern France and afterwards went to study in Paris. Influenced by Jacques Lefèvre d'Etâples he became an evangelical. His preaching was so fearless and outspoken that he quickly drew the attention of the authorities and had to flee the country. Farel went to Basel in 1524 where he was welcomed, but such was his outspoken opposition to Catholicism that he was expelled and went to Strasbourg where he met Martin Bucer. He began to move among the Waldensians (a proto-reformation evangelical group mainly living in what is today Italy) and in 1531 he was instrumental in persuading them to align with the Reformation. The next year found him in Geneva where he worked for the reformation of the city with the blind preacher Courauld and Antoine Froment. Farel was good at demolition, but needed help in the constructive work of reformation, which is why he seized the opportunity to 'persuade' Calvin to stay in Geneva. After their expulsion in 1537 he settled in Neuchâtel where he remained pastor until his death two years after Calvin's. Farel was a powerful evangelist who used every opportunity to preach the gospel. He was one of Calvin's closest friends even though they had their differences, not least when at the age of sixty-nine Farel married the teenage daughter of his housekeeper. Without Farel, Calvin's life would probably have been very different and his impact on the church much less.

William Farel

accepted. In the meantime the Duke of Savoy had laid siege to the city, but when the Bernese army arrived he was defeated in February 1536. Protestant worship was now established in the city's churches.

The city in which Farel had so forcefully persuaded Calvin to stay was very different from the city we see today. Its magnificent location is the same and the cathedral of St Pierre still dominates its centre, but the narrow alleys and jumble of buildings are no longer there, nor are the fortifications that protected the city. As a city state it was self-governing with three councils. The Little Council had 25 members, including the four syndics who administered the city. This Council was elected by the Council of the Two Hundred which was like a city parliament. Its members were elected by the Council of the Whole to which every male citizen belonged. Calvin had to work with the Councils to get his plan for reformation carried through.

Pierre Viret

Beginning the ministry

Farel was by nature a pioneer and realized that he needed help in order to consolidate the Reformation in Geneva. Calvin was just the man. Once Calvin arrived back from Basel he was appointed a 'reader in Holy Scripture'. He had no formal pastoral office and was seen to be a scholar and teacher. He began to lecture on Paul's letters to a small group of students, but soon was undertaking pastoral duties, and within a year Farel was able to persuade the authorities to have Calvin appointed a pastor. Calvin was the regular preacher in St Pierre while Farel preached

Photo by Dr L H Lee

Left: *The old city of Geneva*

in St Gervais across the river. A colloquy, or ministers' meeting, was established where there was exposition and discussion as well accountability to one another.

Within a short time Calvin's abilities were becoming more widely known. In September 1536 he and Farel went to Lausanne, some 65 km (40 miles) away, in order to help Pierre Viret who had become pastor there. A disputation was planned that was intended to help the citizens decide whether or not they would accept the Reformation. Some 300 clergy gathered in the cathedral. Farel and Viret were the main speakers for the Protestants. Calvin had only intended to be an observer, but when one of the Roman Catholic speakers challenged Farel on the teaching of the church fathers on the Lord's Supper, he could not remain silent any longer. With a combination of razor-sharp logical argument and almost perfect recall of passages from early church leaders such as Cyprian, Tertullian, and Augustine he demolished the opposition. The audience was amazed and subsequently around 120 priests and 80 monks became Protestants. Calvin then travelled to Bern to participate in discussions on how to unite the Protestant churches in Switzerland. Bucer in Strasbourg was encouraging the Swiss churches to accept the Form of Concord written in Wittenburg as a basis for unity, but nothing came of it. The reputation of this young lawyer-theologian was growing.

Above: *Rue Jean Calvin, where Calvin's house was located.* *See also page 71*

Reforming the church

Back in Geneva, Calvin and Farel began reorganizing church life. On 10 Nov 1536 they presented the city councils with a confession of faith, followed on 16 January 1537 by a document entitled: 'Articles concerning the Organization of the Church and of Worship at Geneva'. The confession, with its twenty-one articles, was foundational as the reformation of the church had to be built on the truth of the gospel. Some councillors complained that people would be reluctant to sign it, but in the end it was approved. The people were summoned in small groups to come to the cathedral to sign the confession. If anyone refused he or she had to leave the city!

The articles were the key elements of the reformation. First, they stipulated a monthly celebration of the Lord's Supper; Calvin himself favoured a weekly

Above: The pulpit in St Pierre

celebration but, as he pointed out, the danger of the Supper being treated superstitiously convinced him to advocate a monthly celebration. Second, those whose faith or life were contrary to the gospel and who were unrepentant were to be excommunicated; this required a recognized procedure. In addition, they sanctioned congregational singing of psalms, catechetical instruction for children and the revision of laws concerning marriage. The Council took its time, but in the end accepted the confession and the articles. However it added some other laws regulating moral behaviour, and made the Lord's Supper a quarterly celebration. Most arguments in the council were over the Lord's Supper and church discipline; the two were connected and the latter was crucial for Calvin's understanding of the church. The true church was marked not only by the faithful preaching of the word and the correct administration of the sacraments, as Luther and others taught, but also by discipline. Such discipline was not a function of the magistrates, but of the ministers and elders of the church. It was on this issue that Calvin would have most conflict with those in Geneva who opposed him.

However, it was one thing to get the reforms enacted by the Council and another to gain the consent of the people. Morally, many of the people were seen to be very slack, as far as the pastors were concerned; in spite of laws from before the reformation regulating moral behaviour, Geneva was known for its taverns and loose living. Over religion, the population was still divided. Broadly there were four or five groups. Those who still sympathized with the old religion, those who were committed to the Protestant faith, the Libertines who resented the attempts of Calvin and Farel to reform the church and city, the Patriots who resented the Frenchmen having such influence, and the great mass of the people who were caught between the arguments. Increasingly there was grumbling.

However, Calvin and Farel did not only face internal challenges in Geneva. Since it had declared for the Reformation, the city had begun to attract other religious people. Anabaptists, who believed in the complete separation of church and state, arrived, and memories of what happened in Munster some years before when people went wild as some Anabaptists sought to establish God's kingdom, made them unpopular. More significantly for Calvin, in 1537 he disputed with Pierre Caroli, a somewhat erratic Protestant who accused Calvin of not believing in the Trinity and the full deity of Jesus Christ. The occasion for this was Calvin's refusal to sign the Athanasian Creed. There is no doubt about Calvin's orthodoxy, but he disliked the philosophical language of the creed and preferred more biblical language. Caroli's charge outraged Calvin. He went to Lausanne where he defended himself before a synod which decided in his favour, as did a later synod in Bern that also put Caroli out of ministry. Nevertheless rumours persisted of Calvin's unorthodoxy and his enemies used these against him. Meanwhile Calvin pleaded with Viret to join him in Geneva in order to strengthen the cause, but Viret refused.

Below: *The church of St. Gervais*

Photo by Norbert Aepli

Above: Basel

On a personal level Calvin saw his friend du Tillet return to France. The loss of such a good companion must have been felt deeply. It was du Tillet who had told Farel that Calvin was in Geneva. It seems that he was unsettled by the disputes and contrary to expectations, reforming the church was not very easy. In fact there was a deeper issue. Just before he returned to France du Tillet also returned to the Roman Catholic faith and wrote to Calvin to explain his reasons and question whether Calvin was really called to the ministry of the gospel. In part this may have been because Tillet now considered such a ministry illegitimate, but it may also be that he thought Calvin temperamentally unsuited for it. Before du Tillet's letter arrived Calvin had heard of his reconversion and wrote to him. He spoke of how much he missed him and was tormented by the thought that his 'rudeness and incivility' towards him may have moved him to do what he did. Nevertheless Calvin was shocked since 'so sudden a change has appeared very strange to me, seeing the constancy and firmness which you showed.' Calvin could not agree with du Tillet's arguments, but he thanked him for his 'gracious sharing with me of all you had', and asked him for his prayers and assured him of his, that 'the Lord would keep you in His holy protection, and so to direct you that you may not go astray in the slippery path wherein you are.' Without rancour but with deep affection and sorrow Calvin parted with his friend.

Expulsion

The Council elections in February 1538 did not go well for the reformers. Three syndics were elected who opposed Calvin and Farel and the reform programme, and they were told not to exclude anyone from the Lord's Supper. When Calvin and Farel went to protest, they were told to go home. In the meantime the Bernese authorities made a request that certain traditional practices be restored in churches in Geneva. These included baptismal fonts, the use of unleavened bread in the Lord's Supper and the recognition of Christmas, Easter, Ascension and Pentecost. The Council of the Two Hundred agreed, but Calvin and Farel opposed the practices.

Around the same time, Courauld was told not to preach, since his sermons were deemed too critical of the government. When he persisted, soldiers came to arrest him. Courauld had compared the Council to the image of Daniel with feet of clay, and to rats in the straw! Again Calvin and Farel protested. The Council sought a compromise: if Calvin and Farel would agree to Courauld's removal they would postpone the Bernese practices. The reformers refused and the Council ordered that they should not preach either.

It was Easter, and on the streets there were angry crowds and the mood was ugly. On Sunday morning Calvin was in his pulpit in St Pierre and Farel in his at St Gervais. Calvin spoke sorrowfully of how he could not administer the Lord's Supper in such circumstances. In the afternoon, at the church of the Rive, Calvin preached again. As he spoke of the previous events, several men began to shout and with swords tried to storm the pulpit, but sympathizers of Calvin formed a human shield to protect him and

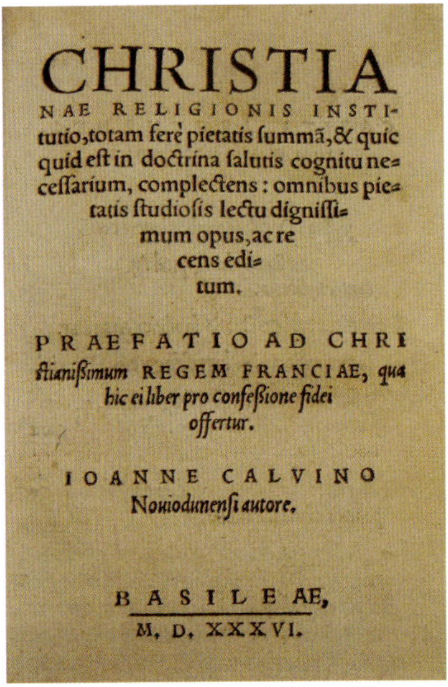

CHRISTIA
NAE RELIGIONIS INSTI-
tutio,totam ferè pietatis ſummã,& quic
quid eſt in doctrina ſalutis cognitu ne=
ceſſarium, complectens: omnibus pie=
tatis ſtudioſis lectu digniſſi=
mum opus,ac re
cens edi=
tum.

PRAEFATIO AD CHRI
ſtianiſſimum REGEM FRANCIAE, qua
hic ei liber pro confeſſione fidei
offertur.

IOANNE CALVINO
Nouiodunenſi autore.

BASILEAE,
M. D. XXXVI.

***Left:** Title page of the 1536 Calvin's* Institutes of the Christian Religion

happily no one was hurt. Late that night the Little Council met and the next day the Council of Two Hundred decided to expel Calvin, Farel and Courauld. They had three days to leave. When Calvin heard the decision he commented, 'Well and good. If we had served men we would have been ill-required, but we serve a good Master who will reward us.'

Above: *Title page of the 1559 edition of* The Institutes

On 25 April 1538 the three reformers set off for Basel. Calvin had spent less than two years in Geneva and was leaving having failed to accomplish what he planned. Who was to blame? Clearly not everyone in Geneva wanted the programme for church reform that Calvin and Farel had proposed. But perhaps they had been too impatient and had not handled their disagreement with the Councils well. Calvin's outbursts of anger would certainly not have helped. Now it looked as if his heart's desire to 'study in privacy in some obscure place' would be fulfilled.

The Institutes of the Christian Religion

Accompanying Calvin all this time was the book that he would become best known for writing, the *Institutes of the Christian Religion*. It is not clear when he began writing it, but he worked on it in Basel and continued to do so in Strasbourg and Geneva until the end of his life. Few books have had a greater impact on the world. It began life as a small book intended as a beginner's guide to the Christian faith. In the preface he wrote that his purpose was 'to transmit certain rudiments by which those touched with any zeal for religion might be shaped in true godliness.' But it was also Calvin's intention that the book would explain and justify the evangelical faith to the French king to whom it was dedicated. The six chapters explained the Ten Commandments, the Apostles' Creed, the Lord's Prayer and the sacraments of baptism and the Lord's Supper. A second edition appeared later in 1536 with additional material on certain doctrines, followed by the third and fourth editions in 1543 and 1550 respectively with considerably more material. The fifth and final edition in Latin appeared in 1559. The book had grown to eighty chapters divided into four sections:

Book One: *The knowledge of God the Creator*. The *Institutes*

opened famously with the words: 'Nearly all the wisdom we possess, that is to say, true and sound wisdom, consists in two parts: the knowledge of God and of ourselves.' Here Calvin explained how we know God through his general revelation in creation and special revelation in Scripture.

Book Two: *The knowledge of God the Redeemer in Christ, first disclosed to the Fathers under the Law, and then to us in the gospel*. Here Calvin explained the Bible's teaching on sin and God's saving grace in the person and work of Christ.

Book Three: *The way in which we receive the grace of Christ: what benefits come to us from it, and what effects follow*. In many ways this was an extended exposition of the biblical teaching of the believer's union with Christ and how the Holy Spirit applies the benefits of Christ's work to his or her life. He dealt with the doctrines of faith, repentance, justification, sanctification, self-denial, Christian liberty, prayer, election, and the final resurrection. This section is a classic of evangelical Christian spirituality well worth reading in itself.

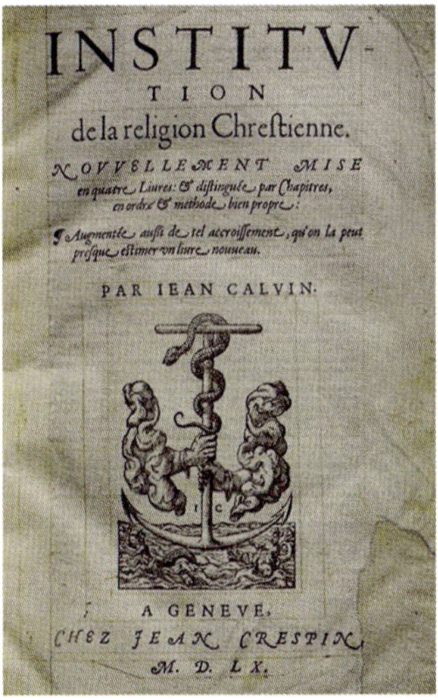
INSTITVTION
de la religion Chreſtienne.
NOVVELLEMENT MISE en quatre Liures: & diſtinguée par Chapitres, en ordre & methode bien propre:
Augmentée auſſi de tel accroiſſement, qu'on la peut preſque eſtimer vn liure nouueau.
PAR IEAN CALVIN.
A GENEVE.
CHEZ IEAN CRESPIN.
M. D. LX.

Above: *French edition of the* Institutes

Book Four: *The external means or aids by which God invites us into the society of Christ and holds us therein*. The visible church was important to Calvin which he called 'the mother of believers'. Refuting the claims of Rome he explained the sacraments of baptism and the Lord's Supper, church government and church discipline. He also explained the role of civil government in God's order.

Calvin wrote the book not only as a handbook of theology and guide to Christian living, but also as a tool with which to study the Bible. Summing up here the Bible's teaching he could more briefly explain the text of Scripture in his commentaries. Such was the popularity of the *Institutes* that within a few years it was being translated and published into many European languages. Indeed its popularity helps to explain the spread of Calvinism. Today it can still be read with great profit.

MAP OF THE OLD TOWN OF GENEVA

1 The Cathedral of St Pierre
2 Calvin's Auditoire
3 The International Museum of the Reformation
4 Rue Jean Calvin and the site of Calvin's house
5 The Hotel de Ville
6 The Reformation Wall
7 The Geneva Academy
8 The Temple Madeleine
9 The Church of St Germain
10 The Church of Gervais
11 Cemetry of Plain Palais (page107)
12 Museum of Art & History

TRAVEL INFORMATION

Geneva

Geneva is the European headquarters of the United Nations, the international headquarters of the Red Cross and the World Council of Churches. From the lake front the famous jet 'd'eau can be seen shooting water high into the air. In Calvin's day the city was much smaller and surrounded by fortifications. The old city is situated on a small hill and is dominated by the Cathedral of St Pierre. If arriving by train from the airport make your way to the Pont de L'Ile and walk up the street that successively is rue de la Cite, Grand Rue and rue de L'Hotel de Ville.

The City Hall (L'Hotel de Ville)

On the right at the top of the hill is the City Hall or L'Hotel de Ville, the historic seat of the city government where Calvin worked and sometimes

battled with the magistrates to establish the Reformation. Through the main gate is an arcaded courtyard some of which dates from the 16th century.

The building contains the Alabama Room where the Geneva Convention was signed in 1864 and the first meetings of the League of Nations were held in 1920.

St Peter's Cathedral (La Cathedral St Pierre)

The cathedral entrance is on the peaceful Cour St Pierre. Construction of the cathedral began in 1160. The neo-classical front was added in 1752. The twin towers and the central steeple are also later additions. The interior is very plain as befits a Protestant church. The impressive pulpit is the one from which Calvin preached. Near its base is 'Calvin's chair'. The Chapelle des Macchabees on the south side dates from 1397 and was restored in 1878. Its decoration gives some impression of what the rest of the interior was like before the Reformation. In the northwest corner is the tomb of Duc Henri de Rohan, a leader of French Protestants a little after Calvin. There is a good view of the city from the main tower. It is also possible to visit the archaeological site underneath the cathedral where you can see evidence of occupation since 350 AD. www.saint-pierre-geneve.ch .

Calvin's Auditoire (Auditoire de Calvin)

Next door to the cathedral is the Auditoire, 1 place la Taconnorie, built as a chapel in the 13th century, where Calvin lectured his students. This was also the meeting place of the English Congregation in Geneva which for a time had John Knox as its pastor. The metrical version of Psalm 100 by William Kethe ('All people that on earth do dwell') set to Louis Bourgeois' tune 'Old Hundreth' was first sung here. Today it is the meeting place of several foreign Reformed congregations, including the Church of Scotland.

Rue Jean Calvin

Opposite the cathedral across the Cour St Pierre is rue Jean Calvin. The site of Calvin's house is on the right marked by a plaque.

International Museum of the Reformation

On the other side of the cathedral on the Cour Saint Pierre is the International Museum of the Reformation in the 18th century Maison Mallet. See chapter 7 for more information.

Other Geneva churches

There are several other churches associated with the Reformation in Geneva. Below the old town on rue Madeleine is the **Temple Madeleine**, today the home of the German Reformed congregation. It has a very simple interior and is the venue for many concerts. **Temple la Fustiere** is on place de la Fustiere on the main shopping street. Across the river Rhone near the main train station is the **Temple de St Gervais** on rue des Terreaux-du-Temple. Farel often preached here. The **Church of St Germain** on rue des Granges near the Hotel de Ville is today an Old Catholic Church, but in Calvin's day was where the congregation of St Pierre would sometimes meet in the winter in order to keep warm.

Au Fantas

4 Strasbourg—city of happiness

Calvin's failure in Geneva was a bitter disappointment. However an opportunity opened in Strasbourg to lead the French congregation there. These were happy years, not least because here he was married. Calvin was also able to learn from what had happened in Geneva

As he made his way to Basel, Calvin must have thought that at last he could devote himself to his studies as he had intended before Farel had persuaded him to stay in Geneva. His efforts to reform the church there had failed, not because they were wrong, but because the Genevans did not want them, and Calvin and Farel had not handled the situation well. Writing later to Farel he confessed, 'Willingly we acknowledge before God…that our unskillfulness…deserved to be chastised.' At first they sought redress from the other church and civil authorities in Switzerland, but the city authorities in Bern and a synod in Zurich did not take their side, and when they tried to return to Geneva the authorities there told them not to enter the city.

Calvin felt he had failed as a pastor and that he must take another course in life: 'After that calamity when my ministry seemed to me to be disastrous and unsuccessful, I made up my mind never again to enter on any ecclesiastical charge whatever unless the Lord should call me to it by a clear and manifest call.' In spite of his vehemence, Farel had been wrong and now Calvin would devote himself to his studies. So together, they made their way to Basel. It was not an easy journey. Writing to Viret, Calvin commented that they reached Basel 'well soaked with the rain and completely spent and worn out.' But in Basel they had friends. For a short time they stayed with John Oporin, who had published Calvin's *Institutes*. However, Farel was soon called to Neuchâtel after the pastor there, Antoine Marcourt, was called to Geneva. Farel wanted Calvin to go with him, but Calvin thought it unwise, as did other pastors. Left in Basel Calvin was 'waiting to understand what the Lord would have me do.'

Photo by Patrik Tschudin

Above: *Basel today*

Facing page: *Petite France in Strasbourg—an area that Calvin would have known*

Invitation to Strasbourg

Calvin did not have long to wait. Martin Bucer wrote to him, asking him to come to Strasbourg to pastor the French-speaking congregation. Early in September 1539 Calvin visited the city, but was understandably reluctant to commit himself after his Genevan experience. At this point Bucer took a leaf from Farel's manual of persuasion and put before Calvin the example of Jonah: 'God will know how to find the rebellious servant, as he found Jonah.' Calvin returned to Basel, but almost before he knew it he was heading for Strasbourg after a 'hurried and disorderly' departure, as he wrote to Farel. On 8 September Calvin preached to the French congregation meeting in the Church of St Nicolas. For a time he lived in Bucer's home which was known as the 'inn of righteousness' because of the hospitality he and his wife Elizabeth gave to so many refugees and others. This was the beginning of three of Calvin's happiest years of ministry—though it did not start like that.

Strasbourg was a German-speaking free city on the border of France. It had early declared for the Reformation and quickly became a centre for the Protestant movement.

Strasbourg Protestantism was peaceable and moderate in tone. The spiritual leaders were Bucer himself, Wolfgang Capito, Matthew Zell and Kaspar Hedio, and they had worked together in Strasbourg since 1523. The leading magistrate was Jakob Sturm who encouraged both religious reform and education. New methods of teaching were pioneered and the city's Gymnasium (school) became renowned. Strasbourg was also very welcoming to strangers and became a refuge for many who were being persecuted, especially in France. For Calvin it was the ideal place. He had the company of Bucer and others, time for study and the opportunity to put into practice some of his ideas on

Top: *Martin Bucer's memorial in St Thomas Church*

Left: *St Thomas Church in Strasbourg where Bucer regularly preached*

church reform. Indeed the system of church discipline and pastoral visitation practiced in Strasbourg was something of a model for what Calvin would later seek to do back in Geneva.

Life was not easy for Calvin in Strasbourg. Early on he was beset by tragedies. Farel's nephew died from the plague; at great risk to himself Calvin took care of him during his illness and he had to write to Farel with the sad news of his death. Then, about a month after arriving, his old colleague in Geneva, the blind preacher Courauld, died in suspicious circumstances in Orde. Courauld's brief pastorate there had been difficult and his death deeply upset Calvin. He wrote to Farel of how: 'The death of Courauld has overwhelmed me, that I can set no bounds to my grief... None of my daily occupations can ... engage my mind....Distress and wretchedness during the day seem only to prepare ...for the more painful and excruciating thoughts of the night', and of having 'these melancholy thoughts all night long.' On top of all this came news from Ferrara that his cousin Pierre Robert or Olivetan who had been serving the Duchess there, had died. He had probably led Calvin to evangelical faith.

However, Calvin's greatest problem was poverty. He had been appointed a 'reader in Holy Scripture' and the city council had voted to pay him, but no steps were taken to execute the decision until several months later, and then it was only a small honorarium that was barely enough to live on. In one letter he wrote, 'I can't call a single penny my own. It is

Top: *Albert Schweitzer's memorial in St Thomas Church*

Left: *The church of St Nicolas, Strasbourg, where the French congregation sometimes met*

La cathédrale, d'après un dessin à la plume de 1548, de Conrad Morant de Bâle, bourgeois de Strasbourg. (p. 307.)

Above: *Strasbourg Cathedral today*

Left: *An old engraving of the Cathedral*

astonishing how money slips away in extraordinary expenses.' Not only did Calvin have his costs of living, but there were outstanding bills from Basel that he and Farel had to settle. Calvin's old friend Louis du Tillet offered to help, but on condition that Calvin did not engage in public ministry. Calvin declined the offer. To make ends meet he may have sold off part of Olivetan's excellent library which he had inherited. When he rented a house he took in boarders and did some private teaching which brought in a little extra income. But he was not a great household manager. Apparently there was some disorder and occasionally he would lose his temper with his lodgers.

But in spite of the deaths and poverty, Calvin was very happy in Strasbourg and seemed set to remain there for some time. Indeed so settled was he that in July 1539 he became a citizen of Strasbourg, for which privilege he had to scrape together twenty florins and to enrol in the guild of tailors. Calvin was not known for his tailoring skills, but guild membership was a requirement for citizenship and for whatever reason he joined the tailors.

Right: *The church of St Madeleine in Strasbourg. The French congregation also met here*

Below: *Martin Bucer's house where Calvin lived for a time*

The French congregation

Among the several reasons for Calvin's happiness was the French congregation. There were between four and six hundred French exiles in Strasbourg, and before Calvin came, there had been no organized church for them, but only occasional preaching. With his appointment, the city council gave permission for the congregation to meet regularly and to celebrate the Lord's Supper. Calvin wrote to Farel: 'For the first time, we have administered the sacrament of the Supper in our little church according to the custom of the place, which we propose to repeat every month.'

Along with the Lord's Supper, Calvin was able to establish a system of church discipline and visitation. In Strasbourg

church discipline was under the authority of city magistrates, but the French church was left to itself and Calvin was able to exercise discipline and pastoral care in the way he thought best. Before the monthly celebration of the Lord's Supper, everyone in the church came to the pastor for questioning. Though Calvin put a great emphasis on church discipline, he was very sensitive and sensible in its application. For example, he was fairly relaxed about what people wore, and when it came to younger members he thought that discipline should not be 'stretched so far that they may not play the fool on some occasion', as he wrote to Farel. Through his preaching and care the church was built up and began attracting even more people. Calvin was particularly able to win over many Anabaptists. One of these was Jean Stordeur with whom Calvin had earlier debated in Geneva.

During his three years in Strasbourg, Calvin had

Worship in the French Congregation

The liturgy of the French congregation drew upon that used by Bucer elsewhere in the city which itself was based upon the Latin Mass of the old church. Its essential elements were:

- An invocation of God's name
- Prayer of confession of sin
- Announcement of absolution
- Singing of the first table of the 10 commandments
- Prayer for forgiveness and strength to keep the law
- Singing of the second table of the 10 commandments
- Prayer for illumination
- Reading of Scripture
- Sermon
- Longer liturgical prayer of supplication and Lord's Prayer
- Singing of the Apostles' Creed or a psalm
- Aaronic benediction (Numbers 6:24–26)

When he returned to Geneva, Calvin developed this liturgy, dropping some things such as the Absolution, and substituting the singing of psalms for the commandments and the Apostles' Creed. He also made more room for extempore prayer. The significance of all this was that Calvin was pioneering the forms of public worship that would become normative in Reformed churches for several centuries and that are still common today. His concern was for the worship to be biblical, but he was not rigid in what he thought was prescriptive; he was relaxed about things such as written prayers and posture. As he wrote to Farel: 'As to trifling ceremonies, strive to induce the brethren not to dispute the point.' Worship had to be sensitive and adapted to its context whilst remaining essentially biblical.

opportunity to put into practice and develop some of his ideas about the church. He established a pattern of public congregational worship that accorded with his understanding of the Bible. In particular he was able to encourage the singing of the psalms which would become a characteristic feature of Reformed worship. He was also able to have lay elders appointed and in addition to being pastor of the church, Calvin taught theology. Most days of the week he would teach students in the choir of the cathedral. This was part of the Gymnasium that Johan Sturm directed where there were not only elementary classes, but more advanced classes in Hebrew, Greek, Latin, mathematics, law and theology. This was a model for the academy that Calvin later established in Geneva. His approach was systematically to expound the Bible, giving the plain sense in its original context and making relevant theological points and applications. He began with the Gospel of John and Paul's letters to the Corinthians, and large numbers attended his lectures.

Singing to the Lord

What struck most people in the worship of Calvin's little congregation at Strasbourg was the singing. Martin Luther loved singing, and hymns played a large role in the Lutheran reformation, many written by him. However, Huldrych Zwingli in Zurich had banished singing from the services, but Calvin disagreed. For him, singing was not only biblical, but it helped to stir the emotions

Above: *Strasbourg street scene*
Opposite center: *Clément Marot*

Left: *The Bouclier church; it is the descendant of the French congregation*

in response to God's truth. The Articles of 1537 that outlined his reforms for the church in Geneva had made provision for singing of psalms. In 1539 he published a small collection of eighteen psalms and three other items. Some were written by him and others by Clement Marot. Marot was an accomplished poet, and as he put more psalms into metrical settings the collection was enlarged and many of Calvin's replaced. Most of what was sung in Strasbourg was psalms, but not everything. Other portions of Scripture such as the Nunc Dimitus (Simeon's Song) were put into metrical verse, and Calvin himself later wrote 'The salutation to Christ' which is still sung in churches. Much as he loved the psalms, Calvin did not think that sung praise should be limited to them; however he did not approve of musical accompaniment to singing since it tended to dominate.

This is how one French speaking refugee was moved by the singing in the Strasbourg congregation:

> 'Everyone sings, men and women, and it is a lovely sight. Each has a music book in his hand ... For five or six days at the beginning as I looked on this little company of exiles, I wept, not for sadness but for joy

to hear them all singing so heartily, and as they sang giving thanks to God that he had led them to a place where his name is glorified. No one could imagine what joy there is in singing the praises and wonders of the Lord in the mother tongue as they were sung here.'

Contending for the faith

From Calvin's teaching came his writing. In spite of recurring illnesses—headaches, indigestion and so on—he wrote a number of books. In addition to the second edition of the *Institutes* published in 1539, he published in 1540 his commentary on Paul's Letter to the Romans which was the first in a long series of commentaries on most of the books of the Bible. This first one established Calvin's reputation as an exegete of the first order which has stood the test of time. Finally Calvin's *Little Tract on the Lord's Supper* was written in 1540, but only later published in Geneva in 1541. Written in French, not Latin, and in non-technical language, it was intended to help ordinary believers to understand the nature of the Lord's Supper. This was a crucial issue in the Reformation. Calvin's theological leadership within what would become the Reformed branch of Protestantism was being established.

In the midst of all this activity Calvin's old adversary Caroli showed up in Strasbourg. Since leaving Geneva Caroli had returned to the Catholic Church, but had now come back to the Protestant faith. He sought out Farel in Neuchâtel and Viret in Lausanne to explain himself. Arriving in Strasbourg in early October 1539, Caroli also sought the approval of ministers with whom he brought up the subject of Calvin's refusal to sign the Athanasian Creed (see chapter 3 for the reason) on which he blamed his reconversion to Rome. Bucer and his colleagues accepted what Caroli said and summoned Calvin to account for himself. They censured Calvin

Above: *Martin Luther*

Right: *Plaque commemorating Calvin as the first pastor the Bouclier church*

Photo by P H Wolfson

Above: *Pretty French city of Strasbourg*

Below: *Philip Melancthon*

and Farel (who wasn't there) for their conduct. Later that night a set of articles was sent round to Calvin's house for him to sign. He refused, and the next day when he met with his colleagues, Calvin lost his temper. At one point he stormed out of the room and Bucer had to come out to calm him down.

Writing of the episode to Farel he confessed that he had 'sinned grievously through not keeping my temper' and on returning home had been 'seized with an extraordinary paroxysm and could find no relief but in tears and sighs.' Nevertheless he would not sign the articles. Farel himself wasn't blameless either, having previously welcomed Caroli. Had he been around, Calvin would have turned on him 'the whole of the fury I poured out on others.' Farel must have been glad that he was in Neuchâtel! Anger was Calvin's besetting sin that he battled with all his life. In the end Calvin's orthodoxy was accepted by his colleagues and Caroli moved on only to return again to the Catholic Church.

Marriage to Idellette de Bure

By the age of thirty, both Calvin and his friends thought that he should get married. As in so many things he confided his thoughts to Farel, writing to him in July 1539 about the kind of wife he wanted: 'I am not of that insane class of lovers who, once captivated by beauty, kiss even its faults. The only comeliness that attracts me is this: that she be modest, complaisant, unostentatious, and likely to be careful for my health.'

Calvin was clearly not a romantic, and was not a little self-centred in his approach to marriage. It comes as no surprise therefore, that his road to marriage was bumpy and went up a couple of dead ends until ending very happily. In Feb 1540 Calvin told Farel that he had been approached by a man and his wife, both devoted to this ministry, who had proposed Calvin's marriage to the man's sister. The proposal looked so good that Calvin asked Farel to preside at the ceremony, but when he asked that the woman learn French she requested time to consider; this, Calvin took as a negative answer and broke off negotiations. Some time later he sent his brother Antoine to ask for the hand of another lady. Again the proposal looked hopeful and again Farel was asked to perform the ceremony. However the woman took several months to give a positive reply during which time Calvin heard things about her that made him break off engagement. At this point he seems to have despaired of getting married: 'I have not yet found a wife, and frequently hesitate as to whether I ought any more to seek one.'

But he did find a wife. On Bucer's advice Calvin married Idelette de Bure, the widow of Jean Stordeur, the Anabaptist whom Calvin had persuaded to join the church in Strasbourg. He had died of the plague leaving his wife and two children. The marriage ceremony was probably conducted by Farel at long last. Idelette was apparently a woman of some force of personality and intelligence as well as being attractive. She was kept busy sorting out Calvin's household, and their lodgers, as well as living on relatively little money.

Wider influence

During his time in Strasbourg, Calvin was able to meet a number of key figures in the Reformation movement. Among them was Philip Melancthon, Luther's younger associate in Wittenburg, with whom he developed a very close friendship. This came about through the attempts of the emperor Charles V to forge an agreement, and possibly reunion, between Protestants and Roman Catholics. Initially, Calvin kept in the background helping to prepare the delegates for the debates, but increasingly he took a more prominent role. On one occasion,

***Top:** A possible portrait of Idelette de Bure*

***Right:** The Rue Calvin in Strasbourg*

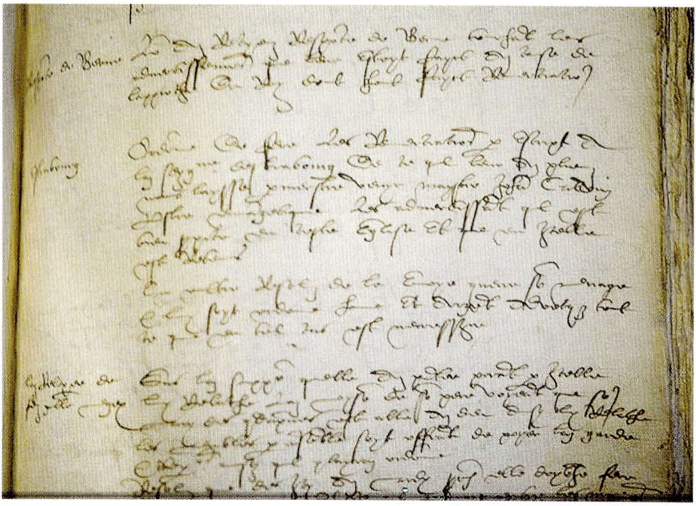

Above: *Geneva council minute recording the decision to invite Calvin to return*

after he had defeated a Roman Catholic theologian in debate, Melancthon gave his friend the nickname 'The Theologian', and at the critical conference at Regensburg Melancthon was keen to have Calvin present because of his 'great reputation among learned men.' Calvin himself was reluctant, but attended nevertheless.

Much as he liked and respected them, Calvin was critical of the tendency of his colleagues to concede too much to their Roman Catholic opponents. Nevertheless he admired their desire for unity, and throughout his life worked hard to achieve it among Protestants. One of the big issues dividing Protestants was the question of how was Christ really present in the Lord's Supper—if he was at all. Calvin argued for a real presence by the Spirit through the faith of those who participated. He talked to Melancthon at length about this and was convinced that he had won him round to his view. Indeed Luther, whom Calvin never met, read his book on the Lord's Supper and commended it, and on one occasion he sent his greetings to Calvin through Bucer. Later, Luther's position on the Lord's Supper hardened, but whatever he thought of Calvin's views Calvin would never speak ill of the great reformer. He wrote: 'Remember what a great man Luther is. Even if he would call me a devil I would yet honour him and call him an illustrious servant of God.'

Involved as he was in high level theological debate, Calvin was always thinking of those who were suffering. One of the reasons he went to these conferences was in order to try to get something done for persecuted Protestants

Photo by Norbert Aepli

Left: Basel today

in France and elsewhere. In part, this could be done if there was an alliance between France and German Protestant princes that might influence the latter to a more favourable attitude. Calvin's efforts in this were commended by Francis I. He also worked for the relief of the suffering of the Waldensians. However, Calvin was also concerned on a more personal level for suffering people. On one occasion when he was away from home, two members of his household died of plague, Claude Feray who was a Greek teacher and his pupil Louis de Richebourg. Calvin's letter to Louis' father reveals his pastoral tenderness. He pointed the grieving father to the sovereignty of God and the work of Christ, but also told him that it was right to 'shed those tears which were due to nature and to fatherly affection' and that not to so grieve would require him 'to put off that common humanity with which God has endowed us.' Needless to say Calvin was also concerned for his own family, but found that while his wife and her children had wisely gone to stay in the country, his brother Antoine had fled to an inn and left his lodgers on their own.

Back to Geneva

Happy as he was in Strasbourg, that city was not to be the focus of Calvin's ministry as a preacher and reformer. While he was at Worms in 1540 two delegates from Geneva approached him and asked if he would return to Geneva as the pastor. His response was to break down in tears! Initially his colleagues at Strasbourg advised him not to commit himself one way or the other, but eventually he was given leave and he knew he had to return. The idea horrified him as he wrote to Farel: 'Whenever I call to mind the wretchedness of my life there, how can it not be but that my very soul must shudder at any proposal for my return?' Geneva had been 'torture' and yet while 'utterly unable to arrive at any settled determination' he was willing, as he wrote to Farel: 'to follow entirely the Lord's calling as soon as he shall have made it plain to me.' After taking advice from friends and others, he decided to return. In the summer of 1541, the Strasbourg city council agreed to let him go for six months, but Calvin was to remain there for the rest of his life.

STRASBOURG

1 The Cathedral
2 St Thomas Church
3 Martin Bucer's house
4 The church of Saint-Nicolas
5 Le Petite France
6 The Historical Museum
7 Bouclier Church
8 The church of St Madeleine
9 St Paul's Church
10 Rue Calvin

TRAVEL INFORMATION

Strasbourg

Located on the Rhine, Strasbourg has always been an international crossroads. Today it is French, but the city has been German and in Calvin's time was an independent city state. A number of European institutions are located here in very modern buildings on the outskirts, including the Council of Europe, the European Court of Human Rights and the European Parliament. The old city is small and situated on an island in the River Ill. The beautiful pink-stoned **Cathedral** with its unusual tower dominates the city. A walk through the old business quarter leads to the **St Thomas' Church** with its Romanesque front and Gothic towers. This is the church where Martin Bucer preached and it has remained a Protestant place of worship since 1549. Both Mozart and Albert Schweitzer played the organ here. Today St Thomas' is a Lutheran church as is the church where Calvin's French congregation mainly met, **Saint-Nicolas-des-Ondes** at 9, quai St

Right: *St Paul's Church, Strasbourg*

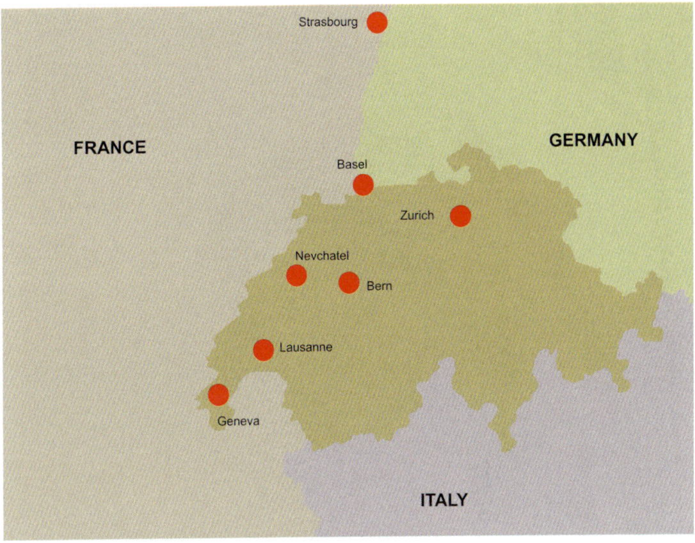

Nicolas. The main Reformed Church is **St Paul's**, an impressive twin-spired building located a short distance north of the old town on a fork in the river at 1 place Eisenhower. Near the University just south of the old town is **rue Calvin** where it is thought Calvin may have lived.

Basel

Calvin spent relatively little time in Basel, but it is worth visiting in its own right as well as for its links with the Reformation. It is a busy port of the River Rhine with a beautiful old city dominated by the Munster or the Cathedral. Built in the 13th century it became a Reformed place of worship at the Reformation under the leadership of Johannes Oecolampadius. The University is the oldest in Switzerland. Erasmus spent time here in the 1530s and 40s and the theologian Karl Barth taught here in the 20th century.

Photo by Luketace

Above: *The European Parliament in Strasbourg*

5 After darkness, light

The thought of returning to Geneva did not appeal to Calvin, but this time he was determined to see the church reformed according to the word of God. There would be opposition, but with God on his side everything was possible

While Calvin had left Geneva, Geneva had never really left Calvin. Although he had become a pastor in Strasbourg, he was still concerned for the flock he had left in the Swiss city. A number of friends from there continued to write to him, and in the autumn of 1539 an opportunity came to help the people. Taking advantage of what had happened in Geneva when Calvin was forced to leave, Cardinal Sadoleto, the bishop of Carpentras in France, wrote to the city and tried to persuade the Genevans to return to Rome. Sadoleto was an upright and scholarly man who wrote commentaries on the Bible and was sympathetic to reform in the church. Someone needed to answer him. After unsuccessfully approaching Pierre Viret in Lausanne, the city officials reluctantly decided to approach Calvin. Already some of Calvin's friends had sent him a copy of Sadaleto's letter and he decided that it was his pastoral duty to answer it. As he explained to a correspondent: 'God, when he charged me with [the pastoral care of the church in Geneva], bound me to be faithful to it for ever. So now I see the worst snares laid for that church, whose safety it has pleased the Lord to make my highest care.'

It took Calvin six days to write what turned out to be one of his finest polemical works. With his rigorous legal mind, Calvin briefly summarized and

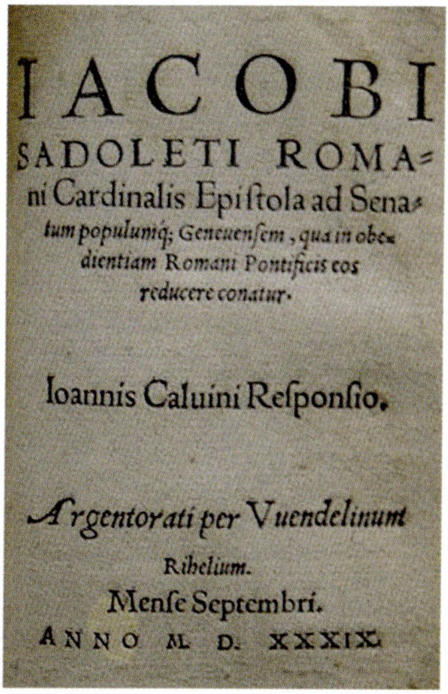
IACOBI
SADOLETI ROMA=
ni Cardinalis Epiſtola ad Sena=
tum populumq; Geneuenſem, qua in obe=
dientiam Romani Pontificis eos
reducere conatur.

Ioannis Caluini Reſponſio.

Argentorati per Vuendelinum
Rihelium.
Menſe Septembri.
ANNO M. D. XXXIX.

Facing page: *The Cathedral of St Pierre where Calvin regularly preached*

Right: *Title page of Calvin's Reply to Sadoleto*

***Right:** The Hotel de Ville in Geneva where Calvin often met with the city authorities*

defended the evangelical faith. Clearly and passionately he answered Sadoleto's charge of heresy and then turned the table on him and charged him with forsaking the teaching not only of the Bible, but of the early church fathers. The Genevans would not forget how Calvin helped them in their time of need.

The attitude of the Genevans towards Calvin was changing for other reasons too. The four ministers in the city were inadequate for the task and lacked the strength of character required to stand up to the city authorities. Before Calvin returned, two of them had left both their charges and the city. The moral life of Geneva was declining and politically there were factions. The Guillermins—named after Farel—were the more sympathetic to Calvin and Farel. Led by Michel Sept they opposed the new ministers and refused to receive Communion from them. Typically, Farel approved of this policy, but Calvin thought it unwise. The Guillermins were opposed by the Artichauds who were more favourably disposed to the policies of Bern and its influence in Geneva. After a considerable struggle, the pro-Bernese party was defeated and new syndics more sympathetic to Calvin were elected. More and more people saw the need for Calvin to return and lead the church. Friends wrote hoping for his return within a year, and Viret also encouraged him to think of returning.

In early September 1540 the Little Council and the Council of Two Hundred agreed to recall Calvin. Outside the city hall people were shouting, 'We must have Calvin'. From Neuchatel,

Farel once again hurled his thunderbolts at Calvin in his letters. On October 23 Calvin replied to the Council with a courteous letter agreeing to come, but identified certain issues that had to be dealt with first. He had responsibilities for the church in Strasbourg as well as other commitments. Writing to Farel he spoke of his willingness to make the sacrifice: 'When I consider that I am not in my own power, I offer my heart a slain victim for a sacrifice to the Lord. ... I yield my soul chained and bound unto obedience to God.' Nevertheless he still dreaded the prospect and told Viret that, 'There is no place under heaven of which I can have a greater dread.' To go to Geneva would be 'to perish daily a thousand times over.' But after his initial reluctance, Calvin had come to see that to return was right. His Strasbourg mentor Martin Bucer agreed to go with him for a short period.

One of the commitments Calvin had to keep before he returned was to go with the Strasbourg delegation to Regensburg for a meeting to discuss the differences between Protestants and Roman Catholics, especially on justification and the Lord's Supper. Calvin was pessimistic about finding an agreement, and left intending to return to Strasbourg in June. While he was away news came of an outbreak of plague in Strasbourg. Happily his wife was spared and he rejoiced at being reunited with her, but some in the church had died and Calvin had to visit many grieving and bereft families. Meanwhile letters kept arriving asking when he was going to return to Geneva. 'Are you waiting for the stones to cry out?' wrote Farel. In early September a Genevan escort

Top: *Calvin's cypher expressing his heart devotion—prompt and sincerely—to God*

Right: *An old engraving of Geneva as Calvin may have known it*

came to bring Calvin back. He re-entered the city on 13 September 1541. Idelette stayed on in Strasbourg for a few weeks until she was sent for when her husband had settled.

Almost immediately upon his arrival, Calvin met with the Little Council. This time its treatment of him was very generous and he was given a new robe, a large house on the rue des Chanoines, a good salary of five hundred florins, as well as annual provision of twelve measures of corn and two casks of wine. A wagon was sent to fetch Idellete and the household. The Calvin family settled into their new home in the upper town near the cathedral. The house was already furnished and there was ample room for the family as well as lodgers and guests; there was also a large garden at the back.

On the first Sunday after his return Calvin preached from the new pulpit that had been built for him. Significantly he picked up in his sermon at the place he had reached before his expulsion! This signalled that for Calvin, what had happened was merely an interruption to his ministry, but even more that he was committed to preaching the word and that his ambition was to bring the people under its authority.

Reforming the church

Calvin's priority was to reform the church in Geneva according to Scripture. He wrote to

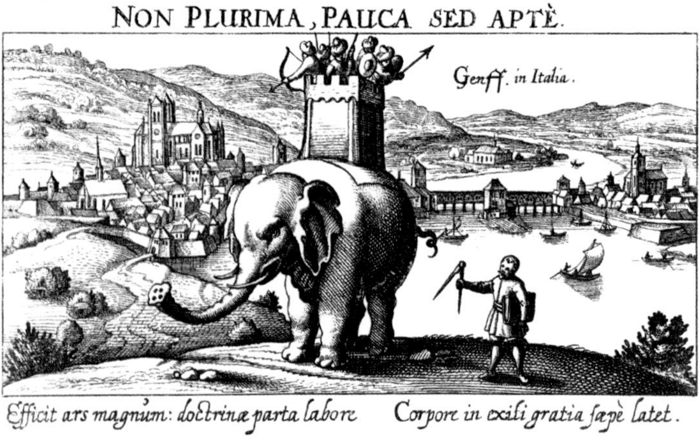

__Above:__ A cartoon attacking Calvin and Geneva. The elephant with thee turbaned Turks in its tower represents the heretics of Geneva being defended by Muslims. The cartoonist may have seen Calvinism as weakening Catholic Europe's defense against the Muslim Ottoman Empire. The image of Geneva in the background is a good impression of the city in Calvin's time. St. Pierre is the large church on the left

Right: *The site of Calvin's house in Rue Jean Calvin*

Farel shortly after his return: 'Immediately after I had offered my services to the Council I declared that a church should be agreed on, such as prescribed for us in the word of God, and such as was in use in the ancient church. Then I touched gently upon certain points...' But Calvin was aware that his approach would have to be less confrontational than last time. He told Bucer back in Strasbourg that, 'Insofar as it depends on me, I shall give ground of offence to no one.' At a service soon after his arrival, Calvin spoke, to the gathered councils and people, of the times in which they found themselves. The Turks had invaded Hungary, there were plagues in several cities, and in France evangelicals were being persecuted. They must look to God for help in such perilous times.

Calvin's programme for reform was set out in the *Ecclesiastical Ordinances of the Church of Geneva* which he submitted to the Little Council on 26 September and which the General Council passed into law without dissent on 20 November. The only substantial alteration to what Calvin wanted was that the Council would retain more authority over the church, even though the church was given significant freedom of action. At the heart of the Ordinances were biblical preaching, church order and discipline. Learning from his mistakes and drawing from his experience in Strasbourg, Calvin began to realize his vision for the church. The greater significance of this is that in the *Ordinances* was the essence of church order not only for Geneva, but for Reformed and particularly Presbyterian churches for centuries to come. Perhaps most significantly he had restored laymen to the government of the church. He was, of course, simply trying to put into practice what he understood the Bible to teach, but he was doing so in line with what the early church had practiced and that the Roman church has forsaken. In this he

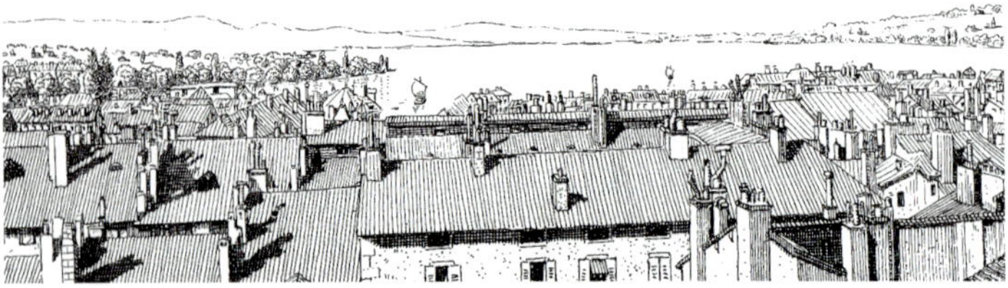

Above: *A view of the rooftops of Geneva from the top of the house on the site of Calvin's home*

had to adapt to the circumstances of Geneva and did not get everything he wanted, but he was able to lay the foundation on which he would build for the rest of his ministry in the city.

It is of course one thing to legislate and another to put into practice, and for this Calvin needed good colleagues. Pierre Viret was with him for the first six months. Calvin desperately wanted him to stay permanently, but the Bernese authorities, under whom Lausanne came, only allowed him a six month extension. Farel decided to stay in Neuchatel. Several of the

A programme of church reform

1. Four orders or offices of the church were recognised: pastor (or minister), doctor (or teacher), elder and deacon. The pastor was to preach the word to the church, administer the sacraments, visit and counsel the people and share in the exercise of discipline. The doctors were to teach doctrine and protect the church from error. Elders were laymen who shared in the discipline of the church. In Geneva the elders were initially members of the Councils, although later some came from outside. With the pastors, the elders formed the consistory that dealt with pastoral and discipline issues. The deacons were charged with visiting the sick and caring for the needy.

2. Preaching was essential. Each Sunday at daybreak there was to be a sermon in St Pierre and St Gervais and then again at nine and at three in the afternoon.
At noon children were to be catechized.
Three sermons would be preached during the week.

3. Baptisms were to be conducted in church and not homes, as was often done. The baptisms were to be near the pulpit. Likewise the table for the Lord's Supper was to be near the pulpit. In order to participate, people came forward in groups and sat at tables.

4. The sick and prisoners were to be visited. The sick were expected to tell ministers in three days that they required a visit.

5. The church was to have power to excommunicate the impenitent. Now, Calvin dealt with it more tactfully. After three warnings offenders would be informed that they must abstain from the Lord's Supper and they would be reported to the Council. Discipline 'should be done with… moderation…for even the corrections are only medicines for bringing back sinners to the Lord.'

other ministers in Geneva Calvin found something of a trial. He complained to one correspondent of them being a hindrance rather than a help and of being 'rude and self-conceited, with no zeal and less learning.' For that reason Calvin felt he had to carry much of the burden of preaching. Eventually however he was able to recruit abler men, especially after the Academy was founded.

An example of the problem Calvin faced was when a plague broke out in the spring of 1542. Calvin was forbidden by the Council from visiting the sick, and only Pierre Blanchet, a French pastor, was willing to do so. Incidentally, a plague at the same time in Strasbourg took Bucer's wife Elizabeth and four of his six children as well as Calvin's former colleague and friend Capito.

Political opposition

Inevitably, it was not long before Calvin encountered opposition to the reforms. There were some who feared that especially in the area of discipline they would affect their freedoms and lifestyle. In 1543 the question of excommunication was raised in the Council. The point of contention was the relationship between the Council and the Consistory. Some insisted that excommunication was the responsibility of Council, whereas Calvin insisted that it was the responsibility of the church.

Above: *The pulpit in St Pierre from which Calvin most often preached*

Photo by Nóbik Attila

Above: *St Pierre where hundreds heard Calvin preach*

When he appeared before the Council to explain his position, Calvin got excited and warned that he would have to be killed or banished before he conceded the point. In the end he got his way, but the issue would rumble on for some years.

At the time, Calvin wondered if there was a plot afoot to undermine his reforms. Certainly by 1545/46 opposition was growing. Much of it centred on several leading and inter-related Genevan families: the Favres, the Bertheliers, the Vandels and the Septs. Accustomed to exercising influence and power in Geneva, they took exception to Calvin as a person and to his programme. The children, who called themselves *les enfants de Geneve,* tended to live on the wilder side of Genevan society. One of them, Philibert Berthelier, liked to interrupt Calvin's sermons with ostentatious coughing. Others would play noisy games outside the church during the service. In time the opposition became known as the Libertines with a leader in Ami Perrin, the sometime Captain-General of the city army. Strangely Perrin had been deputed to bring Calvin from Geneva and had sat on the committee that drew up the Ordinances, but he was now turning against the reformer. In part, this may have been through the influence of his wife, Francesca, a daughter of Gaspard Favre, who disliked Calvin and whom Calvin nicknamed 'Penthesliea'—queen of the Amazons.

Most of the battles between Calvin and the Libertines were over the exercise of discipline by the Consistory. For example, in 1546 Pierre Ameaux was overheard at a dinner party bad-mouthing Calvin as a Frenchman, but worse, accusing him of preaching false doctrine. He was reported and arrested. The Council wanted an apology in private, but Calvin insisted on a public apology since his integrity and that of his colleagues had been attacked. In the end Ameaux was paraded through the streets in an act of humiliation, but a lot of bad feeling had been caused. In the same year Ami Perrin and his wife, as well as other leading citizens, had been found dancing at a wedding reception in contravention of city laws. Initially Perrin refused to appear before the Consistory, but eventually relented after Calvin wrote to him. Calvin's point was that the law had to apply equally to everyone.

By 1547 the opposition was gaining strength, especially after the elections that year gave them a majority among the syndics who ran the city. Then in June, an anonymous note was found in the pulpit of St Pierre that, as well as calling Calvin 'Big pot-belly' and telling him to shut up and stop blaming people, seemed to threaten him with death. Calvin took the threat seriously and reported it to the Council. The police raided the home of Jean Gruet, who was associated with the Favres, and gathered a good deal of incriminating evidence. Questioning revealed that Gruet objected not only to what he considered Calvin's tyranny and the suppression of freedom by the Council, but also that he had been in contact with some foreign power. Gruet was tried and found guilty of several capital crimes and executed in July.

By 1552 the Libertines were able to occupy most of the leading political positions in the city and sought to challenge Calvin and his colleagues on several fronts. In one instance Balthasar Sept, although excommunicated, tried to have his child baptized. At the

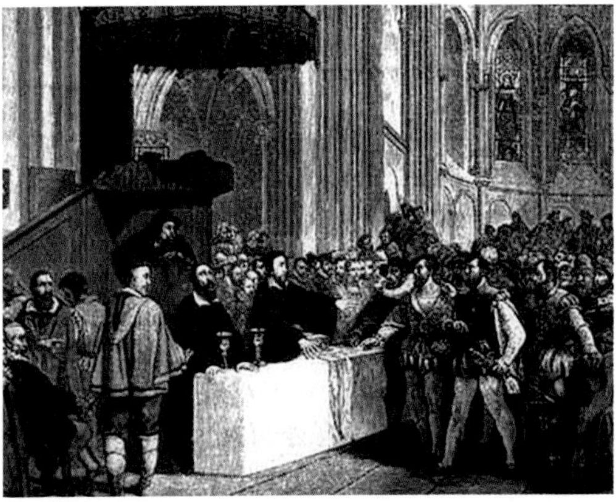

Right: *Calvin turning away the Libertines from the Lord's Supper. The event is probably apocryphal*

CATECHIS-
MVS, SIVE CHRISTIA
NAE RELIGIONIS INSTITV-
tio, cõmunibus renatæ nuper in Euan-
gelio Geneuensis Ecclesiæ suffragijs re-
cepta, & uulgari quidẽ prius idiomate,
nunc uerò Latinè etiam, quo de FIDEI
illius synceritate passim alijs etiam Ec-
clesijs constet, in lucem edita.

IOANNE CALVINO
AVTORE.

BASILEAE, ANNO
M D XXXVIII

Above: *The title page to Calvin's Geneva Catechism*

Easter communion that year the syndics demanded a list of all excommunicated people from the ministers. They refused, and to add insult to injury were also excluded from the General Council to which all citizens were eligible. Calvin was exasperated, and in one letter confessed that 'it is very difficult for me not to boil over when someone gets impassioned.' In May Calvin offered to resign, but the Council refused his request. The Libertines seemed to have got what they wanted. Calvin was humiliated and seemed powerless.

In September the matter of excommunication surfaced again. The issue was whether Philibert Berthelier could be reconciled to the church and receive communion. Calvin insisted that it was a matter for the Consistory to decide, and at the main morning service on the first Sunday of the month warned anyone who was excommunicated not to come to the Lord's Supper. He thought that Berthelier might present himself at the table, but he didn't. Calvin also thought that such was his difference with the Council that he would have to resign, and he preached what was in effect a farewell sermon in the afternoon. In the event the Council decided that in line with the Ordinances, excommunication was the domain of the Consistory.

The Berthelier case rumbled on, but the political winds began to turn Calvin's way. His handling of the Servetus crisis (which we will look at shortly) had made him a champion of orthodoxy around Europe. Then in the February 1555 election, the Libertines were routed and those in favour of Calvin's programme were elected. But what finally defeated the opposition was when in May they tried to seize control of the government in a cack-handed way. At a party hosted by Ami Perrin, several men began to speak against the French residents of the city and to talk of insurrection. Fuelled by drink, a group set off to attack a house where a number of French people lived. In the ensuing confusion Perrin seized the baton of office of a syndic who had arrived to establish order. Perrin was arrested. Shortly afterwards he and a number of other notables fled the city. Calvin's struggle with the Libertines was over.

Theological opposition

However, Calvin faced not only political opposition from within Geneva, but also theological opposition. One of the first cases Calvin had to deal with was also one of the more personally difficult. Sebastien Castellio was the director of the college in Geneva. He was highly respected for his teaching methods and scholarship. However he soon began to disagree with Calvin over several issues. Castellio objected to Calvin's interpretation of the phrase 'descended into hell' in the Apostles' Creed. He also considered the Song of Solomon obscene and questioned its canonical status. In spite of this, Calvin recommended him to teach in Lausanne, but Castellio returned to Geneva. After attacking the Genevan ministers the Council banished him.

More serious was the case of Jerome Bolsec, a former monk who, like Calvin himself, had studied theology in Paris. Bolsec had fled to Geneva from France where he had practiced

Above: *The Servetus monument in Geneva*

Above: *A portrait of Calvin, early middle age. Possibly be Hans Holbien*

as a highly respected doctor. On Friday 16 October 1551 he attended the Congregation, or the gathering of ministers, for discussion and mutual encouragement and admonition. The subject of predestination came up and Bolsec argued against Calvin's position. Among other things he said that the doctrine makes God a tyrant and even an idol. Calvin was not present when Bolsec arrived, but later came in and listened to him. After he had spoken, Calvin addressed the issue. At the end of the meeting Bolsec was arrested, not for speaking against the doctrine of predestination, but for accusing those who taught it of making an idol of God. He was tried, found guilty and banished from the city. Interestingly during the trial, the Genevan authorities consulted other Swiss churches about the issue. Except for

Neuchatel, the others were less concerned about the doctrine of predestination, but all thought that Bolsec was a bad sort. Later Bolsec returned to the Roman faith and wrote a biography of Calvin that virulently attacked its subject and propagated a number of slanders.

The case of Michael Servetus

The case that Calvin has become notorious for is that of Michael Servetus. Servetus arrived in Geneva as a refugee from France where he had been on trial for heresy. Originally from Spain, Servetus was given to theological speculation and had written several books refuting the orthodox doctrine of the Trinity. Fleeing the inquisition he went to Paris where he became a physician with the name of Villaneuve; Servetus then moved to Vienne (about

***Above:** Michael Servetus*

30km south of Lyon) where he practiced his medicine and served as the bishop's physician. He was generally considered a theological troublemaker.

In 1553 Servetus anonymously published a book that consciously mirrored Calvin's *Institutes*. Entitled the *Christianismi Restitutio*, the book called for a wholesale reinterpretation of Christianity in a way that was thoroughly heretical. Servetus was uncovered in Vienne when a French refugee in Geneva wrote to a Catholic relation in the city. The Roman Catholic had pointed out that the evangelicals were heretics, to which the refugee replied that if you want a heretic you need look no further than Servetus in Vienne. He was arrested, tortured and recanted, but still condemned to burn at the stake. However in June 1553 he escaped and made his way to Geneva. Foolishly he attended the morning service in St Pierre to hear Calvin preach and was detected and arrested.

Calvin prepared a charge sheet of theological heresies for which Servetus should be tried. The difficulty for Calvin was that he was in the middle of the worst period of his conflict with the Libertines who were ascendant at the time. His opponents were in charge of the trial and Calvin felt they were using it against him. Servetus himself played on this and used the trial to attack Calvin. In the meantime the council consulted other Swiss cities which were unanimous in their opinion

Above: *Calvin from the Reformation Wall*

that Servetus was a dangerous heretic. The council also wrote to the authorities in Vienne to ascertain what he had been charged with there. The Little Council decided that Servetus was guilty and condemned him to be burnt at the stake. While Calvin approved of the death sentence, he tried to get the form of execution changed to beheading, but to no avail. Servetus was burned at the stake on 27 October 1553. Today many see the Servetus affair as a dark spot on Calvin's life, but at the time he was hailed as a champion of the truth. On this point the Reformed, Lutherans and Roman Catholics agreed. All considered that heresy was dangerous and heretics like Servetus should be put to death. This was, however, the only death for heresy for which Calvin had any responsibility.

On the Reformation Wall in Geneva is the inscription: *Post Tenebras, Lux*—'After Darkness, Light'. The light of the gospel was shining again in Geneva as it was in other parts of Europe. Sometimes things were done that in retrospect were not in line with the message of grace in Christ. But with all his imperfections, Calvin grasped the heart of the matter and did all he could to reform the church according to God's word. For him, this involved not only reorganizing the church but even more, preaching the word that brings light into the darkness.

IHΣ

6 Calvin the man

Calvin saw himself primarily as a preacher and pastor. But what was he like as a preacher and a man? From occasional asides and comments, and the observations of others, we can find an answer to this question

Because of his influence on history, it is easy to forget that Calvin was first and foremost a pastor and preacher of the Bible. He was, of course, actively involved in the civic life of Geneva, and soon after his return he was asked to help reorganize the city statutes in line with the Reformation. His training as a lawyer came in useful. But it was to the work of a pastor that Calvin devoted himself, and in the *Ecclesiastical Ordinances* he described the work involved. Primarily it was 'to proclaim the word of God, to instruct, admonish, exhort and censure, both in public and in private.'

Calvin as a preacher and pastor

Calvin's public ministry of the word was mainly his preaching. It is difficult from this distance in time to appreciate the impact of his preaching on people, but many of those who heard him in Geneva and especially the refugees from France and elsewhere loved it. So devoted were some of these refugees to Calvin's preaching that their organization, the Company of Strangers, employed a full time scribe to record the sermons so that they could be published; for this reason we have so many of Calvin's sermons today. Far from being artefacts from a distant age, they can still be read with value and convey something of the power they had when delivered orally from the pulpit of St Pierre.

What was Calvin like as a preacher? His voice was strong, his diction clear, and he spoke with directness and passion. But it was not his pulpit style that was so compelling; his thought, and the language with which he expressed it was striking. His use of words was especially vivid and he would use colloquialisms

Above: *Calvin preaching in St Pierre*

Facing Page: *Calvin's statue on the Reformation Wall in Geneva*

Above: *Calvin's pulpit in St Pierre*

and illustrations that the congregation would appreciate. Calvin would even verbally dramatize the objections of a hypothetical listener and his response.

It was the intensity of his devotion to the text of Scripture and to communicating its message to the people that was most arresting. Underlying it all was his conviction that in

An example of Calvin's preaching on Christ's ascension from Acts

'Since He has gone up there, and is in heaven for us, let us note that we need not fear to be in this world. It is true that we are subject to so much misery that our condition is pitiable, but at that we need neither be astonished not confine our attention to ourselves. Thus, we look to our Head Who is already in heaven, and say, "Although I am weak, there is Jesus Christ Who is powerful enough to make me stand upright. Although I am feeble, there is Jesus Christ Who is my strength. Although I am full of miseries, Jesus Christ is in immortal glory and what He has will some time be given to me and I shall partake of all His benefits. Yes, the devil is called the prince of this world. But what of it? Jesus Christ holds him in check; for He is King of heaven and earth. There are devils above us in the air who make war against us. But what of it? Jesus Christ rules above, having entire control of the battle. Thus, we need not doubt that He gives us the victory. I am here subject to many changes, which may cause me to lose courage. But what of it? The Son of God is my Head, Who is exempt from all change. I must, then, take confidence in Him." This is how we must look at His Ascension, applying the benefit to ourselves.

A comparison of three great preachers

The following description comes from the pen of a contemporary of the three great friends, Farel, Viret and Calvin:

'… Farel excelled in a certain sublimity of mind, so that nobody could either hear his thunders without trembling, or listen to his most fervent prayers without feeling almost as if they were carried up into heaven. Viret possessed such winning eloquence, that his audience hung upon his lips. But Calvin never spoke without filling the mind of the hearer with the most weighty sentiments. A preacher composed of these three would have been perfect!'

William Farel

preaching, God was speaking as his written word was explained and applied to the hearers. Calvin had a very dynamic understanding of preaching. When a congregation heard a sermon based on the Bible it was, said Calvin, as if it 'heard the very words pronounced by God himself.' Calvin did not think that he or any preacher spoke infallibly, but insofar as they preached the gospel from the Bible, they spoke God's word. That confidence was based on the conviction that the Bible *was* the word of God and that everyone must hear its message so that they can trust Christ for salvation and grow in grace. The preacher's work was simply to unfold God's revelation of his plan of salvation in Scripture and apply it to his hearers.

Calvin was an expository preacher. His practice was to preach through books of the

Above: *Interior of St Pierre*

Bible. He preached directly from the Hebrew or Greek text, without notes, and would take several verses and simply explain them with appropriate application. When his time was over, he would leave off at whatever point he had reached and close with a prayer, picking up at that point in the next sermon. Initially Calvin preached twice on Sunday and then once on Monday, Wednesday and Friday, but in 1542 people asked if he could preach more often! He agreed until other preachers were ready to share the load. Nevertheless that proved too much for him and two months later the council allowed him to preach only once on a Sunday. However, by 1549 Calvin was again preaching twice on Sunday and every day on alternate weeks.

His practice was to preach from a gospel on Sunday mornings and from the Psalms on Sunday afternoons. During the week he preached from the Old Testament. Not surprisingly Calvin had little time to prepare for each sermon. However his preparation for lecturing to theological students meant that he was constantly building his understanding of Scripture and could draw upon it in the pulpit. Where Calvin seems to have prepared himself was in the application of the text. He wrote: 'If I should enter the pulpit without deigning to glance at a book, and should frivolously think to myself, "Oh well, when I preach, God will give me enough to say", and come here without troubling to read or thinking what I ought to declare, and do not carefully consider how I must apply Holy Scripture to the edification of the people, then I should be an arrogant upstart.'

Not least, Calvin prepared *himself*: 'I so speak to the congregation that the teaching must first be addressed to myself.' In fact, he said that he would rather break his neck going up into the pulpit than not be the first to follow what God has said in his word.

Calvin at worship

For Calvin, preaching was at the heart of Christian worship. Drawing upon the liturgy of Martin Bucer in Strasbourg and his own practice there, Calvin developed it for the church in Geneva. In 1542 he published the Geneva service book with the title: *The Form of Ecclesiastical Prayers and Songs ... according to the Custom of the Ancient Church*. Mention of 'the Ancient Church' is a reminder that Calvin saw his reform of

Top: *Clément Marot the poet who put many psalms into metrical form*

worship as not only recovering its biblical shape, but also drawing upon the tradition of the church in the first centuries insofar as it agreed with Scripture. His concern was for the unity of God's people as they gathered to worship him. To this end he sought to encourage congregational participation, particularly through the singing of the psalms. As he wrote in the preface, singing is 'like a spur to incite us to pray and to praise God, to meditate on his works, that we may love, fear, honour, and glorify him.' He thought it best to sing the psalms because: 'When we sing them we are certain that God is putting words in our mouth and they are singing in us to exalt his glory.'

John Knox and 'the most perfect school of Christ'

Of all the English-speaking visitors to Geneva in Calvin's time John Knox was the most notable. Through him, Calvin's ideas took root in Scotland and from there spread to much of the world through migration and missions. Born about 1514 in Haddington near Edinburgh, Knox had an adventurous life. Early on he identified himself with the evangelical movement and as a result spent time as a prisoner on a French galley ship. On his release he went to England where during the short reign of Edward VI the Church of England was being reformed on distinctly Protestant lines. When Mary Tudor came to the throne and sought to return England to the Roman faith, Knox fled to Geneva where he intended to study, but was soon called to the pastorate of the church of English refugees in Frankfurt. He returned to Scotland in 1555 and shortly went back to Geneva, where

The Scottish Reformer John Knox

he wrote a book on predestination and helped to translate and annotate what became known as the Geneva Bible, the version most English-speaking Protestants used until the Authorized Version became more popular. In 1558 Knox was called to become co-pastor of the English congregation in Geneva for which he adapted Calvin's liturgy. Known as the 'Forme of Prayers', this became the template for the simple Reformed or Puritan style of service in many English-speaking churches. Knox's time in Geneva was very happy as this excerpt in a letter to a friend makes clear: 'In my heart I would have wished, yea and can not cease to wish, that it would please God to guide and conduct your self to this place, where I neither fear nor shame to say is the most perfect school of Christ that ever was on the earth since the days of the apostles. In other places I confess Christ to be truly preached; but manners and religion so sincerely reformed, I have not yet seen in any other place.

When Knox finally left Geneva in 1559 he took that vision of a 'sincerely reformed' church and city with him. See in this series *Travel with John Knox* by David Campbell.

In order to be edifying, the hymns as well as everything else in the service, had to be in the language of the people. Helping Calvin to provide the people with psalms in French were the poet Clément Marot and the musician Louis Bourgeois. Marot came to Geneva as a refugee, but stayed only a few years, whereas Bourgeois stayed for sixteen years teaching music.

Important as preaching was, it was only part of Calvin's ministry as a pastor. He regularly visited members of the church and was constantly in demand for pastoral counsel and advice. Prison visitation was also a regular part of his ministry. As we have seen, Calvin was involved in cases of discipline as a member of the Consistory, and he had particular concern for the many refugees that crowded into Geneva, not only from France, but also from England and Wales during the repressive reign of Mary Tudor. He defended them against the sometimes resentful locals and tried to help them practically in relieving distress and hardship.

Top: *A 1602 map of Geneva – The Escalade*

Left: *The Auditoire*

© MIR

Above: *Cartoon of Calvin lecturing on the Old Testament by a student Jacques Bourgoing*

Calvin the teacher and writer

Calvin's public ministry of the word was not confined to preaching. During the week he lectured on the books of the Bible in the Auditoire next door to St Pierre. Calvin was one of the theological professors in Geneva, but perhaps surprisingly did not lecture on what we would call systematic theology, in spite of writing the *Institutes*. His passion was Scripture, and as in his preaching, he worked through books of the Bible. From these came his commentaries that he had begun to publish in Strasbourg in 1540 and continued until the end of his life. His intention was to write commentaries on all Paul's letters, but by the end had also written on much of the Old Testament, the Gospels and all the books of the New Testament except 2nd and 3rd John and Revelation.

In 1546 Calvin experienced every writer's nightmare when the manuscript for the commentary on 2 Corinthians seemed to be lost in the post. It had been sent to Strasbourg where it would be published, but he had not made a second copy. In the event it did arrive, but Calvin learned his lesson and henceforth made second copies. With his *Institutes*, these commentaries stand as Calvin's greatest written legacy to the church. He was one of the greatest exegetes of Scripture in the history of the church, and his purpose of providing help to preachers and others in understanding Scripture is still fulfilled today as his commentaries are widely read.

The *Institutes* continued to be revised, but that and commentaries were only part of Calvin's written works. He also wrote theological treatises on various subjects, and books on matters relating to the church; most of them arose from theological controversies. He wrote about the Lord's Supper (a constant debate of the Reformation), reforming the churches, the Council of Trent, predestination, the veneration of relics, and the Trinity (in the aftermath of the Servetus affair). Some of his writings were of a more pastoral nature. For example, in his *Apologia of John Calvin to the Nicodemites* in 1544 he dealt with the problem of evangelicals who outwardly conformed to the Catholic Church. Some of his compatriots in France felt that he was too rigorous, but Calvin insisted that everyone must conform themselves to the demands of God's word, which for Calvin meant openly confessing the evangelical faith.

Calvin at home

This hard work required considerable self-discipline. Normally Calvin rose at five o'clock in the morning. If he had no other commitments, he would study at home and often did so in bed where his books would be brought to him and where he would dictate letters. Calvin ate little, and one contemporary biographer, Colladon, wrote of his moderation in everything. In part this was due to his constant health problems, but also to a conviction that moderation was to be characteristic of a Christian's lifestyle. There is a legendary story that Bishop Sadoleto once called *incognito* at Calvin's house when passing through Geneva, and was surprised when the man himself opened the door and at the humbleness of his living conditions. True or not, Calvin could speak of how he 'delighted in a life of poverty'. In fact, he refused his last quarter's stipend before his death because he felt he hadn't earned it.

While little concerned for his material comforts, Calvin had a great love of the beauty of creation as the almost lyrical passages in the *Institutes* bear witness. Not surprisingly Calvin was fond of walking in the gardens around the city and visiting the country home of his brother Antoine. Like many naturally reserved people, Calvin was known to his friends for a sense of humour and particularly a love of puns that the wider public rarely saw. He occasionally played a game of bowls, an indoor game similar to modern ten pin bowling, and outdoors he was known to enjoy quoits.

The house where Calvin lived no longer stands, but its site is marked by a plaque on a house on the rue Jean Calvin near the cathedral. The house belonged to the city as did its contents. It was large, and afforded ample room not only for Calvin's

Left: *Interior of the Auditoire where during the week Calvin lectured on the Bible*

immediate family, but also for a time for his brother Antoine and his family, lodgers and the constant stream of visitors. Idellete had her hands full with the management of such a large household and the constant demands of hospitality, but there were some servants, including the hunchedbacked Pierre Daguet.

We know little of Calvin's home life with Idelette. They had two children, both of whom died in infancy. The first was a boy named Jacques who was born prematurely in 1542. Calvin had just returned home from Lausanne and wrote to his friend Viret about his anxiety: 'My wife has been delivered prematurely, not without danger; may the Lord have care over us.' Jacques was baptized, but died two weeks later. Writing again to Viret, Calvin spoke of how 'the Lord has certainly inflicted a severe and bitter wound in the death of our infant son. But he is himself a father, and knows what is good for his children.' Naturally the loss was always painful, as we see in his reply years later to an opponent who ridiculed him for not having children. He replied, 'God had given me a son. God has taken my little boy....But I have myriads of sons throughout the Christian world.' A daughter died at birth in 1545. Idelette's daughter Judith from her previous marriage lived with them. However, Antoine's four children would have filled the house with noise and activity.

Above: *Gardens in Geneva with the famous floral clock*

Idelette's death

Idelette never enjoyed good health and periodically suffered bouts of illness. We do not know what she suffered from, but apparently there was much coughing which suggests that it might have been tuberculosis, and by 1548 she was getting worse. Writing to Viret, Calvin spoke of how she was 'so overpowered with her sickness that she can scarcely support herself.' By early 1549 Idelette often could not leave her bed, and at the same time Calvin was embroiled in his disputes with the Libertines as well as with a myriad of other problems inside and outside Geneva. Three days before her death, Idelette spoke of her trust in God and how she had committed her children to the Lord. On the 29th March, a minister visited to comfort her when she suddenly cried out, 'O glorious resurrection, O God of Abraham, and of all our fathers, in thee the faithful trusted during so many past ages, and none of them have trusted in vain. I too will hope.' Later she added, 'Let us pray; let us pray. All pray for me.' Calvin spoke

Left: *Plaque at site of Calvin's house*

to her of Christ and of their marriage and prayed with her. An hour later at 8 o'clock in the evening Idelette died peacefully.

Calvin was deeply upset by Idelette's death. He maintained his public ministry and continued to preach and lecture almost every day. But to friends his grief was visible. Writing to Viret he confided, 'Truly mine is no common grief. I have been bereaved of the best friend of my life, of one who, if it had been so ordained, would willingly have shared not only my poverty but also my death.' To Farel he wrote, 'I do what I can to keep myself from being overwhelmed with grief. ... May the Lord Jesus support me ... under this heavy affliction, which would certainly have overcome me, had not he, who raises up the prostrate, strengthens the weak, and refreshes the weary, stretched forth his hand from heaven to me.'

Calvin never remarried. A year after Idelette's death he wrote that he was committed to a solitary life. In a personal aside in a sermon on 1 Timothy he explained why that was right. He did not want anyone to think him virtuous for not being married. 'I know my infirmity', he said to a congregation that must have pricked up its ears, 'that perhaps a woman might not be happy with me. However that may be, I abstain from marriage in order that I may be more free to serve God.' What did Calvin think the infirmity was?

Although Idelette had died, there was still a household for Calvin to care for and that in time brought him much heartache. In 1548 Antoine's wife was accused of adultery, though she was subsequently exonerated. However in 1557 it became clear that she had committed adultery with the household servant Pierre Daguet. Antoine divorced his wife and Calvin had to handle the difficult pastoral situation that had arisen in his own home. It was also discovered that Daguet had been stealing from the family. A few years later Calvin's stepdaughter Judith was also found to have committed adultery.

Postage stamp with a possible likeness of Idelette de Bure

A circle of friends

However if Calvin's domestic life was less than happy after Idelette's death, he had a wide circle of friends. The closest were Farel and Viret. They were constantly corresponding with one another and occasionally were able to meet. Like all good friends, their relationship was occasionally tested. The biggest test came in 1558 when Farel, until then a bachelor, announced that he was planning to marry a woman much younger, by many decades, than himself. Calvin wrote expressing his disapproval. But more often they supported each other in the difficult times of life. When Viret's first wife died in 1546 Calvin wrote to invite him to come quickly to Geneva so that he could 'gather heart again with us.' On another occasion Calvin undertook to find Farel a new housekeeper and to find Viret a second wife. Calvin the matchmaker is not a common image of the stern reformer!

When he heard that Farel was dying, Calvin travelled to Neuchatel to see him one last time. As it happened, Farel recovered and lived for some years more. As token of their friendship, Calvin dedicated his commentary on Titus to him. Writing eight months after Idelette's death he wrote, 'I do not think that there has ever been, in ordinary life, a circle of friends so sincerely bound to each other as we have been in our ministry.... I have been a fellow pastor here with both of you; and so far was there from being any appearance of envy, that you and I appeared as one.'

There were other friends as well. A number of friends from previous years had come to live in Geneva. Next door to Calvin was Nicolas Cop who had delivered the famous address as rector of Sorbonne that sparked such controversy (see page 23). Francois Bude, the son of the great French humanist and with whose family in Paris Calvin had been so familiar, also lived in Geneva with his mother and brothers and sisters. There were also friends from Noyon such as Laurent de Normandie, now a wealthy publisher who lived next to the cathedral, and the de Hangest brothers with whom Calvin had been to school and studied at university. Another friend was the French printer Robert Estienne, also known as Stephanus, who had moved to Geneva in 1550 with his business; he printed many of Calvin's books. Among Calvin's closest friends in Geneva were Falais, or Jacques du Bourgogne, and his wife. When he became a Protestant, Falais, a diplomat with aristocratic connections, wrote to Calvin for advice. Eventually he and his wife came to Geneva where Calvin tried to find them a house. Calvin dedicated his commentary on 1 Corinthians to Falais who was a devotee of Calvin's writings. Apparently Falais became so absorbed in the book that he ignored his wife, and Calvin wrote to her counselling patience as her husband 'enjoys himself all alone reading my commentary.'

Top: *Calvin's cup. Probably a gift from his friend Laurent de Normandie*
Above: *'The Candlestick' shows the unity of Protestantism. Calvin is to its right and Luther to its left. 17th century*

TRAVEL INFORMATION

Neuchâtel

The city where Farel spent the remainder of his life after being expelled from Geneva is a very attractive town, perhaps the most distinctively French in Switzerland. It is about 100 km northeast of Geneva in the Jura region. There is a statue of Farel in front of the city's Collegiate Church where he was minister. The church is a fine example of early Gothic with a plain Protestant interior.

Lausanne

In the course of his career Calvin made a number of visits to Lausanne, about 50 km north-east of Geneva along the northern shore of Lake Geneva. His friend Pierre Viret was the senior minister here and preached regularly in the cathedral, considered the finest Gothic church building in Switzerland. There are hourly trains from Geneva. Along the way the small lakeside town of Nyon, also visited by Calvin, is a pleasant place to visit.

Top: *Cathedral on a hill in Lausanne*
Above: *Neuchâtel today*

Photo by Loulou

7 'A city set on a hill'

People came to Geneva from all over Europe, not only as refugees from persecution, but also to see how a church and city could be reformed by the word of God. When Calvin died, his influence would not die with him

About a month after Idelette died, Theodore Beza arrived in Geneva as a refugee from France. He was from an aristocratic family whose ancestral home was in Vezaley, and had met Calvin when Beza was only twelve and they lodged in the same house in Bourges. What influence, spiritual or theological, Calvin had on the precociously bright boy we do not know, but later during a serious illness, Beza came to evangelical faith. Like Calvin, he had to flee into exile and made his way to Geneva. There he stayed a short time—although long enough to be married by Calvin—and moved to Lausanne where he became professor of Greek in the academy. In 1559 he returned to Geneva as a pastor and rector of the new academy, and now his friendship with Calvin deepened and he became Calvin's right hand man.

Beza was only one of many who took refuge in Geneva from the persecution of the Church of Rome. They arrived from Italy, Spain, the Netherlands, England, Scotland and elsewhere. The majority, like Beza, came from France and for whom French-speaking Geneva was a natural haven. Some of the leading refugees we have already noted as friends of Calvin, but there were many other ordinary people who had to abandon homes and livelihoods for a precarious life of exile. At one point a thousand refugees were arriving every year, and during this time the houses in Geneva became notably taller as floors were added to them. The indigenous population was not always happy with this development and there were inevitable tensions. However, the refugees often brought skills, enterprise and connections

Facing page: *Geneva today*
Center: *Beza as a young man*

Above: *The church of the Fustieres is the descendant of the French congregation in Geneva*

Left: *Auditoire where some of the foreign congregations met*

with them that benefited Geneva's economy.

For his part Calvin tried to help the refugees practically. He was able to convince the Council to establish a cloth-making factory, and also established congregations in the native languages of the refugees. In time, the refugees themselves established an organization, the Company of Strangers, to represent their needs. They were among Calvin's greatest supporters in Geneva, and it was the Company that paid for a secretary to take down Calvin's sermons so that they could be published.

One of the refugee congregations was English-speaking. During the reign of Mary Tudor from 1553 to 1558, many Protestants fled to the continent and some of them settled in Geneva. Among the English refugees was William Whittingham, future dean of Durham, and John Bodley, whose son would later found the Bodleian Library at Oxford, and most notably John Knox whom we met in the previous chapter. The congregation gathered for worship on Sundays in the Auditoire where Calvin lectured during the week. Today the Auditoire is the home of several expatriate congregations including that of the Church of Scotland.

International influence

Calvin's international influence extended beyond the refugee communities in Geneva. His concern was to see evangelicals across Europe united in faith, and to this end he maintained a wide-ranging correspondence with a vast array of church and civil leaders. Until his death in 1560

Calvin wrote occasionally to Philip Melanchthon, Martin Luther's younger colleague and successor in Wittenburg. He was especially concerned to bridge the divide that was opening up between the Lutheran church and what would become the Reformed church. Among the latter was Heinrich Bullinger in Zurich. Calvin and Bullinger corresponded often, and while not as close a friend as Farel or Viret, Bullinger got on well with Calvin and they worked together for the unity of the evangelical churches in Switzerland and beyond. Their positions on the Lord's Supper were slightly different, but for Calvin, who taught that Christ was spiritually present in the Lord's Supper in a fuller sense than Bullinger, 'we will not, on that account, cease to hold the same Christ, and to be one with him.' Not long after Idelette died, Calvin travelled with Farel to Zurich to discuss the matter with Bullinger and other leaders. Out of it came the Zurich Consensus on the Lord's Supper of 1559 and after Calvin's death the Helvetic Confession of 1566.

Heinrich Bullinger

Wherever he thought his influence could be brought to bear for the Reformation, Calvin wrote letters. So there are letters to King Sigismund II August of Poland where Reformed Christianity was growing in the towns and among the aristocracy. He wrote to German princes such as Frederick III, the elector of Palatine, and Philip of Hesse; there were also letters to theologians and leaders such as the Pole Jan a Lasco, the Italians Peter Vermigli, Ochino and Zanchi, and Germans such as Hedio, Sturm, and Olevianus.

Calvin had a particular concern for England, and after Edward VI came to the throne he began a correspondence with the Lord Protector, the Duke of Somerset, encouraging him in his policy of reform. The Duke valued

Photo by Ikiwaner

***Left:** Zurich where the Reformation was pioneered in Switzerland and where Bullinger was leading pastor*

Above: The short-lived Protestant King of England, Edward VI

Calvin's writings and apparently his wife sent Calvin a ring as a token of their appreciation. Calvin dedicated his commentary on I Timothy to Somerset. To the King himself Calvin sent copies of his commentaries on Isaiah, James, Peter, John and Jude, and dedicated them to him as 'a truly Christian Prince'. Later he also sent Edward a short collection of sermons. In the accompanying letter he wrote to Edward: 'It is indeed a great thing to be a king and … over such a country, but have no doubt that you reckon it beyond comparison better to be a Christian.' Calvin encouraged Edward to see himself as an English Josiah.

Calvin also corresponded with other English leaders such as Miles Coverdale, Edmund Grindal, John Hooper and not least with Thomas Cranmer, the Archbishop of Canterbury. Calvin and Cranmer shared a common passion for Protestant unity. The Roman Catholic Council of Trent had begun to meet and it was imperative that there was a united Protestant front. Cranmer wrote in 1552 to Calvin, Melanchthon and Bullinger proposing a synod or conference: 'Shall we neglect to call together a godly synod … for restoring and propagating the truth?' he asked. Calvin replied that 'So much does this concern me that, could I be of any service, I would not grudge to cross even ten seas, if need were on account of it …' Sadly nothing came of the proposal since Edward died in 1553 and Cranmer and many others were shortly to be martyred in Mary's cruel reign. Nevertheless Calvin's influence grew in England through the exiles that came to Geneva, and even more through the impact of his writings that were being published in English.

What many people needed was counsel about how to deal with the rising persecution. In 1543 he wrote his *Petit Traicte* (Little Tract) in which he urged people who could not flee, to abstain from idolatry, by which he meant the Roman Mass. Of course to do so would invite persecution, but Calvin felt that Christians had no option if they were to live in conformity with the gospel. Many felt this counsel was too hard and Calvin replied in his *Excuse…a Messieurs les Nicodemites* that Christians must not be like Nicodemus who came to Jesus by night, but rather openly confess their faith and accept the consequences.

However Calvin was much more closely involved than merely writing books. He wrote letters to many who were suffering and most notably in 1552 to 'the five scholars of Lausanne'. These were five young Frenchmen who had studied under Beza and Viret in Lausanne and had returned to France where they had been arrested in Lyon. As they waited in prison for the appeal process to be completed, Calvin counselled them as a caring pastor with unsentimental tenderness and firmness. As release seemed increasingly unlikely they must prepare themselves by prayer and trust God for the grace to endure this trial: 'So, my brothers, be confident that you will be strengthened according to your need by the Spirit of our Lord Jesus, so that you will no more faint under the heavy weight of temptations than did he who won such a glorious victory that in the midst of our miseries it is an unfailing pledge of triumph.'

The five scholars were only some of the young men who were trained in Geneva and Lausanne as ministers of the word, many of whom returned to France. In parts of the country, groups of evangelicals were meeting, and by the 1550s some of these groups were becoming churches. The Paris church was in existence in 1555 and others were soon established in Orleans, Bourges, Angers, Tours, Poitiers, Rouen and many other places. By 1559 there were at least seventy-two Reformed churches in France, and in 1559 the first synod of the French Protestant churches was convened in Paris. Calvin did not actually approve of this step at this stage, but the synod went ahead and adopted his church polity and a confession of faith that was modelled on the Genevan confession. To these churches men from Geneva came as pastors and evangelists. It is estimated that between 1555 and 1566 around one hundred and twenty men were sent from Geneva to France. One of the key ways in which the evangelical faith was promoted was through literature that was printed in Geneva and smuggled into France and distributed. Unsurprisingly, the French government did not like

Photo © Christian Richard

Above: *Cambridge where many of English Calvinists studied*

Right: *Thomas Cranmer, Archbishop of Canterbury and correspondent with Calvin*

Above: The original building of the Geneva Academy

this and put pressure on Geneva to stop it, but as it was the work of the Company of Pastors and not the Council they absolved themselves of any responsibility. In the subsequent decades the French churches would multiply to over a thousand.

The Academy

From the beginning, Calvin had envisaged an academy for

Calvin's heart for France

Understandably Calvin's heart was with the growing evangelical movement in his native France. Initially evangelicals were persecuted sporadically under Francis I, but under his son Henry II, who acceded to the throne in 1542, the persecution was intensified. The growth of the movement increasingly seemed to threaten the state. While many fled, others stayed and suffered. It is estimated that during the 42 years of both reigns, 50,000 evangelicals were put to death in France. What happened in France in the 1540s was far worse than anything that happened in England under Mary Tudor.

Calvin sought to deal with the situation by several means. He worked hard to gather practical support from the Swiss churches, and he addressed the kings themselves. Famously the *Institutes* was dedicated to Francis and in part was aimed at justifying the evangelical faith to the king. Calvin wrote to various individuals such as Admiral Gaspard de Coligny and Margaret of Navarre who might be able to influence events. Coligny had converted to the evangelical faith and was only one of the more prominent examples of an increasing trend among the aristocracy. As explained in the *Institutes*, Calvin thought that people in certain official positions should use their power to check injustice.

training men for the ministry of the word. There was a college in Geneva, but it was not at the level Calvin wanted. For many years theological teaching mainly consisted of the lectures that Calvin and others gave to interested students. In 1558 the Council took steps to establish an academy. After a dinner in late March the syndics invited Calvin, and whoever else was interested, to accompany them to a site on the northern edge of the city. It was agreed to build a college with six lecture rooms. The foundation stone was laid later that year but, because of lack of funds it wasn't completed until 1563. The original building can still be seen in the Bourg-du-Four district behind the cathedral.

In the meantime, Calvin began to recruit professors. He wanted his old teacher from Paris, Mathurin Cordier, to head the academy, but Cordier chose to stay in Lausanne. Other leading scholars who were contacted also declined. In the end Calvin persuaded Theodore Beza to become rector. Beza was relatively young, but he had begun to make his mark as a theologian and teacher and in a few years would become one of the leading theologians in Europe. At the same time that Beza was appointed, all of his colleagues decided to decamp to Geneva because of political issues in Lausanne. Not only did the new academy gain a ready-made faculty, but as the students came with them it gained a student body as well.

The academy was opened with a service in St Pierre on 5 June 1559. It was led by Calvin who also addressed the congregation about the purpose of the academy. Beza gave a lecture on the history of education beginning with the patriarchs. Although the academy would eventually become the University of Geneva, it began as both a secondary school and theological seminary. The former was called the *schola*

***Above:** The burning at the stake of Ann de Bourg in Paris; one of many evangelicals martyred in France during Calvin's lifetime*

Above: *St Bartholomew Massacre Painting in Geneva*

privata and aimed to ground its pupils in humane learning, particularly the classical languages and Hebrew, with a view to progressing to university status. Within five years the lower school had a thousand students. The higher school was called the *schola publica* which offered theological education, and within five years it had 300 students. Here was taught not only doctrine, Greek, and Hebrew, but also philosophy, logic, rhetoric (the art of communications), physical sciences and mathematics. Because of the fame of Calvin and his colleagues, students came from all over Europe and especially from France, to which many returned as pastors. The academy embodied Calvin's ideal of a learned ministry equipped with the skills necessary for faithfully preaching the word.

Calvin's last years

After the final rout of his opponents in 1555 Calvin's life was relatively peaceful. He continued to preach, lecture, visit people in need, counsel, participate in various meetings, write letters, edit his commentaries and much else. He had never enjoyed robust health, but his closing years were marked by a number of illnesses. He suffered occasional bouts of fever as well as stones, gout and piles, and increasingly serious pulmonary tuberculosis. His coughing affected his preaching, and in the last two years of his life Calvin was often carried from his house to the church in a chair or on horseback.

Writing to his friend Bullinger in Zurich in April 1564 he admitted the poor state of his weakening body: 'Although the pain in my side is abated, my lungs are so full of phlegm that my breathing is difficult and short. A stone in my bladder has been very troublesome for the last twelve days. Add to that our anxiety, for all remedies have so far proved ineffectual. Horse-riding would have been best, but an ulcer in the haemorrhoid vein tortures me when sitting down or lying in bed, so that I could not bear the agitation of riding. Within the last three days the gout has been very troublesome. You will not be surprised, then, if so many sufferings make me lazy. I can hardly be brought to take any food. The taste of wine is bitter.'

By the time he wrote to Bullinger in April, Calvin had not preached since February and would never preach again. On Wednesday 2 February he had lectured for the sixty-fifth time on the book of Ezekiel, but had to stay at home for the rest of the week. On the Sunday he preached for the last time in St Pierre. However, it was becoming clear to everyone that he was a seriously ill man. Occasionally Calvin would venture out to the Friday meeting for ministers or

Photo by Sylenius

Above: *The University of Geneva—the descendant of Calvin's Academy*

attend a service in St Pierre, and on one occasion to address the Council. But increasingly any exertion exhausted him. At home he would meet with people, work on a revision of the French New Testament and continue to deal with his correspondence. When admonished to work less he replied, 'What! Would you have the Lord find me idle when he comes?'

But Calvin knew he was dying. He made a will in late April in which he left what money he had to various family members and the Academy and Company of Strangers. On 27 April the Little Council visited him. Calvin thanked them for their efforts with him in advancing the reformation in Geneva, and apologized both for not being able to do all he could have done and for his bad temper that had too often been expressed in his dealings with them. He exhorted them to trust God and to do his will for the people of Geneva.

Above: *Calvin as an old man*

The ministers of the city came the next day. He felt very weak and thought he might not be able to say what he wanted to say. Calvin reminisced about what Geneva had been like when he arrived all those years ago: 'When I first came to the Church, I found almost nothing in it. There was preaching and that was all. They would look for idols, it is true and burn them. But there was no reformation; everything was in disorder. There was, of course, the good man, Maistre Guillaume [Farel], and then blind Courald. And besides them there was Maistre Antoine Saunier and that fine preacher Froment, who laid aside his apron and got up in the pulpit, then went back to his shop, where he chattered, and thus gave a double sermon.' The initial struggles, the expulsion and then the battle for reformation after his return were recounted. There had been physical dangers as when dogs were set on him and shots were fired on one occasion: 'Just imagine how that frightened a poor scholar, timid as I am, and I confess I have always been.'

With perhaps more than a little self-pity Calvin spoke of the slanders and ill health he had suffered during his life, but he was more than aware of his faults: 'But certainly I can say this, that I have willed what is good, that my vices have always displeased me, and that the root of the fear of God has been in my heart; and you may say that the disposition was good; and I pray you, that the evil will be

Above: *Calvin meeting with his colleagues for the last time*

forgiven me, and if there was any good, that you conform yourselves to it and make it an example. As to my doctrine, I have taught faithfully, and God has given me grace to write what I have written as faithfully as it was in my power. I have not falsified a single passage of the Scriptures, nor given it a wrong interpretation to the best of my knowledge; and though I might have introduced subtle senses...I cast that temptation under my feet and always aimed at simplicity.'

Calvin commended Theodore Beza to his colleagues as his successor: 'Take care of him, for the charge is great, and so weighty that he might well sink under the load.' They were to care for the church and also for the city and not to become factious or to bicker among themselves. Perhaps surprisingly for someone who had during his life made some radical changes, he told his colleagues not to make any since 'all changes are dangerous and sometimes hurtful.' However, what Calvin meant was that the Reformation was not to be undone even with the best of intentions.

Calvin lived for another month. Before he died he was able to write a letter to his old friend Farel that brings together many of the themes of Calvin's life: his confidence in God's sovereign care, the importance of friendship, his consideration of others, his devotion to Christ and his quiet hope of glory: 'Since it is God's will that you should outlive me, remember our friendship. It was useful to God's church and its fruits await us in heaven. I do not want you to tire yourself on my account. I draw my breath with difficulty and expect each moment to breathe my last. It is enough that I live for Christ, who is to all his followers a gain both in life and in death.'

On 27 May 1564 at 8 o'clock in the evening Calvin died: 'Gone to God whole and entire in sense and understanding, thanks be to God' as the Council register recorded the event. Calvin had requested that he be buried in an unmarked grave and, after his lying in state for a few days, the request was fulfilled. Today there is a stone marked with the name of John Calvin, but it is only conjecture that that is where his body lies awaiting the resurrection for which he so fervently hoped in life.

Genva and Switzerland after Calvin

After Calvin's death the leadership of the churches was taken by Theodore Beza, and for several decades the city remained a centre for Reformed theological education. One of its most famous theologians was Francois Turretin, one of several theologians in the family which originally came from Italy. Sadly, in the 18th century

Theodore Beza

Genevan Protestantism became increasingly rationalistic and drifted far from Calvin's theology, becoming deistic and some pastors even denied the deity of Christ. In the early 19th century there was a revival of orthodox Calvinism in Geneva known as the Reveil, in which several theological students were converted and became leaders of evangelical movements in other parts of Europe. One of them, Merle d'Aubigne, wrote a monumental history of the Reformation. The Scottish preacher Robert Haldane was involved in this revival when he spent time in Geneva.

Above: *The cemetery of Plainpalais where Calvin is buried*

TRAVEL INFORMATION

Geneva

The Geneva Academy

Rue Theodore de Beze

Behind the cathedral is the atmospheric Bourg-de-Four neighbourhood at the far end of which is the original building of the Geneva Academy that became the University of Geneva. The building is part of the university which is now spread to other parts of the city.

Museum of Art and History

2, rue Charles Galland

In addition to its superb archaeological and art collections there are some historical exhibits relating to Geneva in Calvin's time.

Calvin's Grave?

Heading west along the Boulevard Saint Georges is the Cimetiere de Plainpalais. We know that Calvin was buried in this cemetery, but there is no certainty as to the exact location of his grave. At the far end close to the southern wall is a gravestone marked with the initials 'JC' that some think is the grave. The entrance to the cemetery is on rue des Rois. Sir Humphrey Davy, the inventor of the miners' lamp, is buried here.

The Reformation Wall (Mur de la Reformation)

Parc les Bastions

Below the rue de la Croix Rouge is the Parc des Bastions in which is located the magnificent Reformation Wall or more formally, the International Monument to the Reformation. Construction began in 1909 at the commemoration of the 400th anniversary of Calvin's birth. It stretches for 100 metres along what were the old city walls. In the centre are four five metre high statues of Calvin, Farel, Theodore Beza and John Knox. Along the wall there are other reliefs of important Protestant leaders such as Martin Luther, Huldrych Zwingli, Oliver Cromwell, William of Orange and Roger Williams as well as engravings of important Protestant texts. Over the heads of the central statues are the words in Latin *Post Tenebras Lux*—After the Darkness, Light.

Photo by Dr.L.H.Lee

Above: *Traditional grave of John Calvin in Geneva*

8 To the ends of the earth

Calvin left very few possessions when he died, however his theological, ecclesiastical and cultural legacy is great. Calvinism has proved itself adaptable to different cultures, and around the world his legacy has left its imprint

Calvin's legacy is spread across a number of areas of life and on many continents of the world. While his greatest legacy was in theology and church life, the influence of his ideas is seen in areas such as politics, education, economics, science and the arts. His thinking contributed not only to the Reformation of the church, but also the development of the modern world. The French historian Emile Leonard wrote, 'Calvin invented a new kind of man in Geneva—Reformation man—and in him sketched out what has become modern civilization.' What is Reformation man? Someone who lives consciously before God under his sovereign rule. This is the 'Old English Puritan' described by John Geree in 1646 who was 'such an one, that honoured God above all, and under God gave everyone his due. His first care was to serve God, and therein he did not what was good in his own, but in God's sight, making the word of God the rule of his worship.' Even when the Calvinism that created that kind of man at his best has waned, the sturdy independence of conscience and concern for doing what is right remains in societies influenced by Calvinism. However Calvin could not conceive of life apart from knowing the God revealed in the Bible. In this chapter we will take up different strands of the story of Calvin's life and explore his legacy today.

Not everyone sees Calvin's legacy in a positive light. He is sometimes caricatured as a tyrant who established a theocratic dictatorship in Geneva. However it is clear from the historical evidence that this was far from the case. The city authorities were firmly in control of what happened in

Facing page: *The Congregational Church in Woodstock, Connecticut, illustrates the simplicity of the Calvinistic approach to art*

Right: *Calvin's* Institutes *have been one of the vehicles of his legacy*

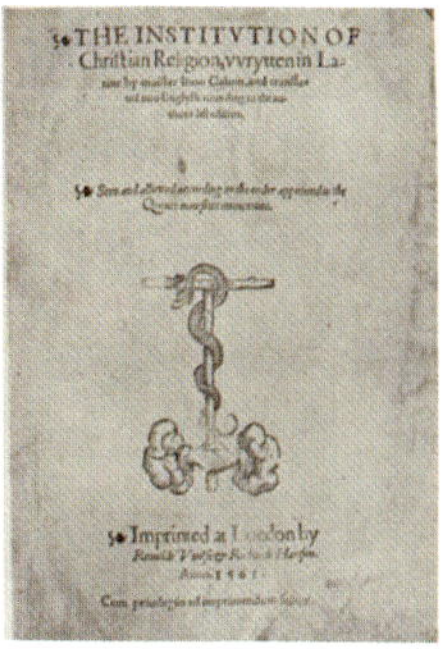

Geneva and very often Calvin did not get his own way with them. Many of the laws that sought to control public and private morality predated his coming to the city and were not unusual at the time in other cities, Protestant and Roman Catholic. In Europe at this time there was a fear of social disorder and Calvin believed, like most people, that government had a role in controlling how people behaved. It is also significant than he was not made a citizen of the city until later in his life. Nevertheless he had great influence in Geneva and sought through his preaching and influence to make it a godly society.

Theologically many disagree with his doctrine of predestination, and more generally his critics have accused him and his followers of wanting to establish a theocracy, being censorious, humourless, heresy hunting and much more. Of course neither Calvin nor his legacy is without blemish. Some of Calvin's personal failings have been mentioned in previous chapters, and it is also true, as a Hungarian proverb puts it, that some of those who have claimed to follow him have been better Calvinists than Christians. Too many have fought for a cause or a form of theology without having the deep personal piety that was so important to Calvin himself. While we must strive for the ideal we will always fall short. We must also remember that Calvin was a man of his times and that while he understood many things, clearly he had his blind spots. That is true of those who follow him in every generation. Many Calvinists have, in spite of their theology and

Right: *The Victorian Baptist preacher C H Spurgeon loved Calvin and his theology and was delighted to preach in his pulpit on a visit to Geneva: 'I preached in the cathedral at Geneva; and I thought it a honour to be allowed to stand in the pulpit of John Calvin … I do love that man of God; suffering all his life long, enduring not only persecutions from without but a complication of disorders from within, and yet serving his Master with all his heart.'*

Above: *The Westminster Assembly of Divines (1643–1649) that promoted the Presbyterian church order that was adopted in Scotland*

even their personal devotion to Christ, tolerated and sometimes perpetrated great evils. But happily with Calvin's God there is always grace for the worst of sinners.

Calvinism

The theological system that bears his name, Calvinism, has been one of the most formative in the history of the church. Calvin was convinced that he was simply teaching what the Bible said in agreement with the best of the church's teaching through the centuries. However, he had a remarkable ability for bringing together much that others had taught and then distilling and expressing it in a fresh way that deepened theological understanding.

He was a master communicator of both the spoken and written word, which accounts for much of his influence. Contrary to what many think, he was not obsessed with the idea of predestination, although like many of his day he believed that it was the Bible's teaching. In fact he saw it not as a matter of speculation, but of assurance and comfort. There is no doubt though that Calvin was passionate about the glory of God and his sovereignty as Creator and Redeemer.

In all that he wrote, whether his commentaries on the Bible or his theological works, Calvin sought to centre the lives of Christians on the God who has graciously spoken in Scripture and redeemed his people in Jesus Christ. Calvin's theology is spiritually rich and biblically balanced. He is, as the American theologian B B Warfield concluded, the church's great theologian of the Holy Spirit. That may surprise many, but to Calvin there could be no Christianity without the Holy Spirit since it is his work to apply to people what Christ accomplished and to open their eyes to the truth. It is the spirituality of Calvin's theology and its largeness of vision that has made it so compelling. Others taught most of what he taught, but it was the way he brought it all together and followed through its practical implications for individual Christians, the church and the world that made Calvinism such an enduring legacy.

There is an ongoing debate as to the extent Calvin's successors faithfully transmitted or subtly changed some aspects of his theology, but that doesn't diminish his legacy. The Puritans in 17th century England and Holland owed much to Calvin's theology as, in different circumstances, they sought to answer new questions when faced with new challenges. In the 18th century leaders such as George Whitefield and Jonathan Edwards evangelistically and intellectually sought to relate Calvin's legacy to their times just as C H Spurgeon, Thomas Chalmers, Charles Hodge, Herman Bavinck, J C Ryle and many others sought to do the same thing in the 19th century. In the 20th century theologians and preachers such as J Gresham Machen, D M Lloyd-Jones, J I Packer, Karl Barth and Thomas Torrance among many others, have identified themselves with Calvin's theological legacy. Today, Protestants in many denominations call themselves Calvinists and in many parts of the world there is a resurgence in Calvinist theology. That does not mean they follow his teaching in every detail. For example, there are many Baptists who are Calvinists but who disagree with Calvin's approval of infant baptism; they nevertheless agree with him on his understanding of God's sovereignty in salvation.

Presbyterianism

Calvin was not only a great preacher and theologian, but also a great organizer. He did not set out to establish a new denomination,

Calvinism and Arminianism

In the 17th century Jacobus Arminius, a Reformed theologian in Leiden in the Netherlands, questioned Calvin's doctrine of election. To refute his teaching an international synod was convened in Dordrecht (Dort) that restated a Calvinistic understanding of grace. The well-known English acronym TULIP is derived from the Canons of Dort and is an attempt to summarize the doctrine of God's sovereign grace in salvation.

T—total depravity. Human beings are radically sinful and cannot save themselves.

U—unconditional election. God's choice of sinners to be saved is not because of any foreseen faith or good works.

L—limited atonement. Christ's death while sufficient to save all was designed to save those whom God has chosen.

I—irresistible grace. God's saving grace cannot in the end be resisted by those whom he will save.

P—perseverance of the saints. Those who have believed in Christ will persevere to glory.

Some Reformed theologians such as Moises Amyrald who taught at Saumur in France in the 17th century disagreed with the doctrine of limited atonement and considered it out of line with Calvin's teaching. However, most orthodox Reformed theologians have agreed with the Canons of Dort.

but because he was called to reform the church in Geneva, he went back to the Bible and sought to put into practice what he understood it to teach about the church. His *Ecclesiastical Ordinances* for the church in Geneva was the result, but his thinking can be found in many of his writings. For Calvin the church was essential for the Christian life, and he spoke of it as the mother of believers. He agreed with Martin Luther that the marks of a true church were the faithful preaching of the word and the administration of the sacraments of baptism and the Lord's Supper. But Calvin added that the discipline of church members was also essential if the church was to retain its integrity. Calvin believed that Reformation was not only a matter of doctrine but also of church life. The whole life and work of the church, and particularly its government and worship, was to be governed by the word of God. However Calvin was not pedantic and he allowed for considerable variations according to local circumstances and cultures. For example, in corresponding with leaders of the Church of England he advised them to tolerate certain aspects of the liturgy that more radical Protestants wanted removed. This twofold emphasis on church discipline and the regulation of church life by Scripture became a distinctive of what became known as the Reformed churches.

Calvin's thinking about church government contained the seeds of what has become known as Presbyterianism. In Geneva the local churches were connected together through the Company of Pastors. This was a meeting where pastors and elders met to discuss issues, examine candidates for ministry, exercise discipline and coordinate action. As the number of churches in France grew, a system developed in which local churches were governed by councils of elders made up of ministers and lay leaders that were

Above: *Orchard Road Presbyterian Church in Singapore, established by Scottish Presbyterians during the period of the British Empire*

Above: *Oliver Cromwell's statue outside the Palace of Westminster in London*

Photo ©2008 Pilise Gábon

linked regionally and nationally for the purposes of accountability and cooperation.

This system proved remarkably adaptable in very different circumstances and cultures and spread to many places where leaders followed Calvin's theology. One example is Scotland where John Knox, the pioneer Reformer who had spent time in Geneva, sought to reform the Scottish church along these lines. There were similar developments in the Netherlands, parts of Germany, Poland, eastern Hungary and Transylvania in present-day Romania. Since then Presbyterianism has spread all over the world as, for example, Scottish and Scotch-Irish emigrants to North America brought their Presbyterianism with them. Presbyterianism is a major denominational tradition in the United States and Canada which in turn has been taken by missionaries to Africa, Asia and Latin America. Something similar happened with Dutch and German emigrants. Calvin's essential Presbyterianism has proven to be remarkably adaptable to very different cultures and circumstances. Today some of the largest Presbyterian churches are found in South Korea, Indonesia, Southern Africa and Kenya.

Government and politics

Calvin's impact is not only theological and ecclesiastical. One area where his influence is still felt is in government. Nations in which there have been significant numbers of Calvinists have been strongly influenced by him even after their influence has waned. Based on his understanding of the Bible's teaching, Calvin believed that government was ordained by God for the good of society and therefore involvement in politics was a divine calling. Nevertheless, because of his doctrine of sin and understanding of fallen human nature, Calvin knew that too much power was easily abused and therefore he was wary of high concentrations of political power. Three aspects of Calvin's thinking about government have had a lasting and beneficial impact on the modern world. First, the authority of government is limited in scope. In preaching from 1 Samuel 8 Calvin claimed: '...there are limits prescribed by God to a [king's] power.' In part this is because of the spiritual independence of the church. Under God the church and state have two separate though related spheres of responsibility. While ideally working in partnership (as was the case in Geneva) the state must not interfere with the affairs of the church. Many of the struggles for liberty, especially in the English-speaking world, have been on this issue.

Second, Calvin believed that government power should be separated between the different branches of government and there should be elections by citizens for public office as was the case in Geneva. He preferred a republican form of government to a monarchy, but what mattered was that there were checks and balances on power. In time Calvin's position was recognized in the British Glorious Revolution of 1688 and the American Constitution, through the influence of thinkers influenced by Calvin's ideas such as John Milton and John Locke. Today we take them for granted. Calvin was not a modern democrat and as the Servetus case showed he did not share modern ideas of toleration, but the seeds of what we know as pluralistic democracy are found in his thinking.

Third, Calvin taught that there is a place for resistance to government tyranny. All Christians have an obligation to submit to government authority and in general Calvin advised persecuted Christians to resist passively by obeying God and accepting the consequences. However he did allow for government officials to resist tyranny in line with their responsibilities. So, for example, a judge must decide a case according to the law and not the dictate of a king.

After his death some of Calvin's followers developed this idea into a doctrine of active resistance in which citizens could rebel against a tyrant and even overthrow him. The development of Calvin's teaching later played a significant role in the English and American Revolutions. Not surprisingly Calvinists have been very active in political affairs. The political thinking and activity of statesmen such as Oliver Cromwell (the Lord Protector) in 17th century England, John Witherspoon (one of the founding fathers and a signer of the Declaration of Independence) in the United States in the 18th century and Abraham Kuyper in the Netherlands in the 19th century were shaped by their Calvinism. Where Calvinism has been influential, people have generally lived in societies of ordered

Above: *Abraham Kuyper—Dutch pastor, journalist, educator and politician*

freedom in which inner restraint and character are more important than laws and force of arms.

Work and economics

Calvin's teaching on the dignity and divine calling of 'secular' work enabled people to see common human activity in a new light. Not only the work of the clergy but that of farmers, merchants, doctors, teachers, soldiers, politicians, housewives and others legitimately employed is a vocation that could be devoted to the glory of God. In his teaching on keeping the Sabbath, Calvin taught that not only should time be set aside in the course of a week for public worship and physical rest, but also that the work of the other six days of the week was itself important. In a sense Calvin taught that all work was sacred activity. One of the great contributions of Calvinism in line with that of Protestantism in general to the modern world has been its dignifying of work.

It was his positive understanding of work that more than anything else in Calvin's teaching contributed to the development of modern market economics. It has been wrongly claimed that Calvin taught that economic success is a sign of divine election. In fact he said that it was 'an error ... to look upon those who are oppressed with afflictions as condemned and reprobate' and to make 'judgments about the favour of God from an uncertain and transitory state of prosperity.' Calvin disliked excessive luxury and in his writing and preaching warned Christians of its dangers. His personal life was an example of simple living. More importantly it was sinful to become rich at the expense of the poor. Christians must not 'grow rich by injustice, nor to plunder [their] neighbour of his goods' nor 'hasten ... to heap up wealth cruelly wrung from the blood of others ...'

At times Calvin sounds like Karl Marx. However, for Calvin there is nothing wrong with making money, and he encouraged people to do so by honest labour and enterprise. While not an important part of his teaching Calvin did not think that lending money at a modest amount of interest was wrong, but that excessive interest rates were, and this is what he considered usury. Here Calvin was moving away from the teaching of the medieval Catholic Church.

Significantly, Geneva itself during and after Calvin's time became an increasingly important centre of trade and banking. Whereas when Calvin arrived in the city there were some fifty

Photo by diliff

Above: *The City of London—Britain's financial centre*

Photo by Magnus Manske

Above: *Emmanuel College Cambridge where many English Puritans studied*

merchants, by the 1650s there were one hundred and eighty as well as over one hundred printers and publishers. Calvin's influence in this area was part of a larger movement in Europe that saw cities gaining greater influence, as well as the development of banking and international trade.

Social Welfare

Calvin's concern for the poor was not merely a matter of theory or exhortation from the pulpit. An essential part of his reform of the church in Geneva was the provision of deacons who had particular responsibility for the practical care of people in need. In the Catholic Church the office of deacon had become a lower order of the clergy, but with Calvin it became a lay ministry for social welfare. The deacons in Geneva provided financial assistance to the poor, work training, loans for setting up businesses, care for widows and orphans and medical care. Under Calvin's leadership a new hospital was established that provided both medical care for the sick and accommodation for the destitute. In addition to this there was a fund for helping poor refugees.

Between 1550 and 1560 some 60,000 refugees passed through Geneva. Money was raised both from the citizens of Geneva as well as from outside. Calvin also encouraged the different nationalities among the refugees to help themselves through committees. The office of deacon was imitated in other Reformed churches inspired by Calvin's example. Today in Europe many of the responsibilities of the deacons in Geneva have been taken over by the state. That in itself is a tribute to Calvin's legacy in this area, but there are still many social needs that churches still try to meet through diaconal ministries.

Education

Calvin was concerned for the general as well as the religious education of children. The Academy that he persuaded the city to establish in 1559 became a model of education for Europe. It was divided into two sections. The *schola privata* was a combination of what we would see today as a secondary school and an

Photo by billyau84

***Above:** Harvard University founded by Puritans*

undergraduate college. This was to provide a general education. Beginning with 280 students, by 1564 when Calvin died, twelve hundred students were enrolled. After Calvin's death, under Theodore Beza's leadership departments of law and medicine were added. The *schola publica* is what today would be called a theological college or seminary. This was intended for training ministers not only for the churches in Geneva, but also in France and elsewhere in Europe. Calvin's academy became a model for education in Protestant countries. For example, in Scotland John Knox sought to follow the example of Geneva by aiming to establish a school in every parish. In time this led to Scotland becoming one of the most literate countries in the world. Later in the 19th century Abraham Kuyper in the Netherlands led the development of a network of Christian schools. He also followed Calvin's example in founding the Free University of Amsterdam. In other countries Calvinists have done the same thing. Edinburgh University in Scotland and Emmanuel College in Cambridge University in England were founded in the aftermath of the Reformation. Harvard, Yale and Princeton universities in the United States, as well as many other institutions of higher education around the world, are the result of Calvin's vision in Geneva. The same is true of the many theological colleges specifically devoted to the training of ministers.

Art and Music

Calvin's legacy in the arts is often considered negligible if non-existent, but that is not true. It is true that Calvin disapproved of paintings in churches and that Reformed churches did not patronize art in the way the Catholic Church did. This was due in part to a desire to avoid superstition, but also to a positive desire to enhance the simplicity and spirituality of public worship. Nevertheless Calvin's attitude allowed for the development of 'secular' art in the sense of art for other than strictly religious reasons. His love of creation inspired the development of painting that celebrated the beauty of nature and ordinary life as seen particularly in the great 17th century Dutch artists. Painters such as Rembrandt took up biblical themes, but in a way that brought out the humanity and even ordinariness of his subjects. Calvinist churches may not have had the elaborate décor of Catholic or Lutheran ones, but the 'simplicity, sobriety and measure' (Donald Davie) that characterized them and indeed anything Calvinist is something beautiful in itself. The austere simplicity of an 18th century New England Congregational church is an example of this. There was no place for traditional church music in Calvinist services, but Calvin's encouragement of congregational singing of the psalms contributed, along with Luther's hymn-writing, to a new kind of church music. It is significant that the Lutheran Johann Sebastian Bach's non-religious Brandenburg Concertos were written while he was serving in the court of a Calvinist prince. It is also recognized that jazz in part has its roots in the psalm singing that originated in Geneva, and that black slaves in the southern states learned from Scots settlers.

The written word

Because of the centrality of the Bible in Calvin's thinking it is understandable that his legacy in literature and publishing would be considerable. He was an excellent writer in French

Above: *An 18th century engraving of the Geneva Academy by Pierre Escuyer (1809)*

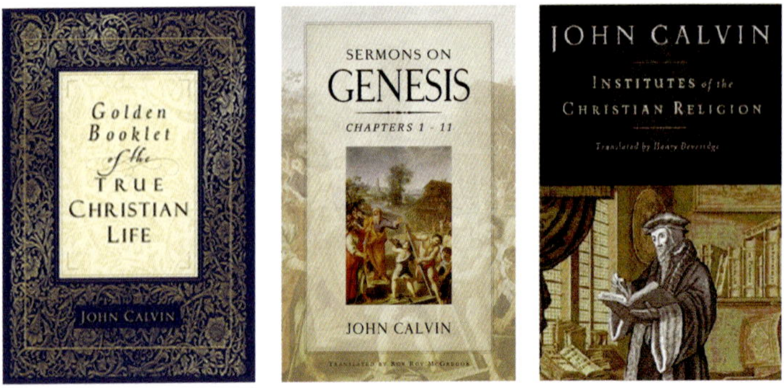

Above: *Some of Calvin's books today*

and he is considered one of the most formative influences in the development of the French language. His writings were published in many other languages. This was possible because of the developments in print technology which began a century earlier with Gutenburg's invention of the printing press. Like Luther and the other Reformers, Calvin took full advantage of this development in order to advance the cause of the Reformation and through his influence Geneva became a centre for publishing. There were 34 presses at work in Geneva in 1563. Calvin's friend and neighbour Laurent de Normandie (also a native of Noyon) became an important publisher and developed a European book distribution network. While Calvin's own writings were published in great numbers, other authors and materials were as well. The Genevan psalm book was a particular publishing success. In the year 1562 alone 27,400 copies were printed in Geneva most of which were exported elsewhere. Calvin is also considered one of the most important influences in the development of French as a literary language. From Geneva also came the Geneva Bible that was used by and influenced the English Puritans, the Pilgrim Fathers and Shakespeare.

Science

One of the striking things in Calvin's writings is his almost lyrical celebration of nature. Calvin's love of creation was also shared by many others in Protestant countries, Calvinists and otherwise, who were at the forefront of the development

Photo by Kaibsu Tai

Above: *The home of the Royal Society in London*

of science. It has been noted by historians that until the 19th century, Protestants were relatively more numerous in scientific activity. In the Academie des Sciences in France between 1666 and 1883 Protestants, although a small minority, outnumbered Roman Catholics. When the Royal Society was founded in England in 1663 sixty-two percent of its members were of Puritan origins. In addition to this love of nature, Calvin's teaching on creation and providence, as well as on the importance of stewardship of God's gifts and the responsibility of Christians to glorify God, contributed to an attitude conducive to scientific enterprise. Another factor was Calvin's emphasis on the authority of the Bible which encouraged people to criticize prevailing ideas in science. Nations influenced by Protestant and Reformed views have historically led the world in scientific and engineering advance.

Calvin's legacy in France

Calvin's longing was that his native France would be won for the evangelical faith. As well as training and sending ministers to preach and to encourage and care for evangelical believers, his counsel was often sought by evangelical leaders such as Gaspard de Coligny, Admiral of France. Faced with persecution Calvin counselled French Protestants to be faithful and not to resist with violence. However towards the end of his life some were talking of armed resistance to tyranny. In 1562 the first war of religion broke out and although it ended before Calvin died, there were other wars over the next thirty years. The most infamous atrocity in this dark period was on 24 August 1572, St Bartholomew's Day, when many notables had gathered in Paris for the wedding of the sister of Charles IX to the Protestant Prince Henry of Navarre. At the instigation of his mother, Catherine de Medici, the king ordered the killing of Protestants in Paris and other cities. Thousands lost their lives including Admiral de Coligny and the philosopher Pierre Ramus. The conflicts ended only with the signing of the Edict of Nantes in 1598 after which there was relative religious freedom. Protestants in France, who became known as Huguenots, (a word of uncertain origin), were very influential in many areas of French life. Nevertheless, over the next decades their freedoms were slowly eroded until in 1685 Louis XIV revoked the Edict accompanied by persecution of such ferocity that thousands of Protestants fled into exile in Germany, the Netherlands, England, Ireland, North America and South Africa. The 18th century was a very difficult time for French Protestantism and is often called 'The Church in the Desert'. Public worship was forbidden and so, secretly people would meet in remote places where pastors would preach to them and serve the Lord's Supper. It was only with the French Revolution that Protestants regained their freedom.

Huguenot memorial in South Africa

TRAVEL INFORMATION

Geneva

See page 48 for the map of Geneva

International Museum of the Reformation (Musée International de la Reforme)

4, rue du Cloitre

This excellent museum must be visited. It is housed in a beautiful 18th century mansion next to St Pierre and is filled with informative and attractively displayed exhibits. In the courtyard is a striking sculpture of a Huguenot cross. The elegant rooms on the ground floor are each dedicated to various aspects of the history of the Reformation in general and Calvinism in particular. There are fascinating displays of cartoons, Bibles, first editions of important texts, domestic and ecclesiastical artefacts and much more. The Grand Salon has an interesting interactive introduction in several languages. The Theological Banquet is a simulated debate on election between key figures in Genevan history, beginning with Calvin and ending with Jean Jacques Rousseau. In the tiny room dedicated to music, various psalms and hymns can be heard. The museum also has a shop and café.
Website: www.musee-reforme.ch/english-version

Above: *The salon of the museum*
Top: *The International Museum of the Reformation*

Among the many interesting things to see in Geneva are the **International Museum of the Red Cross** and the **Palais des Nations**. The former is located at 17, avenue de la Paix in the international area about 1km north of the main train station overlooking Lake Geneva. This superb museum has a number of displays relating to international conflicts and the work of the Red Cross. The nearby Palais des Nations was the headquarters of the League of Nations from 1929 to 1936. After the founding of the United Nations, the complex became its European headquarters and the offices of a number of agencies. There are tours of the art deco building.

FRANCE

Around France there are a number of museums dedicated to the history of French Protestantism.
For more information about museums and historic Protestant churches
see: www.temples.free.fr and www.museeprotestant.org .
Among the best is the **Musée du Desert** near Anduze. This fascinating museum is in a reconstructed Protestant village in the Cevannes. This area has historically been a Protestant stronghold. Many of the local towns and villages have large Protestant temples. The temple in nearby Anduze is the largest Protestant church in France. The museum is particularly strong on the period of persecution after the Revocation of the Edict of Nantes known as 'Le Desert'.
www.museeedudesert.com
Le Mas Soubayran, 30140 Mialet, Gard.

Photo by Yann Forget

Photo by Jacques Martin

Above: *Palais des Nations—the European United Nations headquarters in Geneva*

Right: *Musée de Desert*

Time line of the life of John Calvin

There is dispute about some of the dates relating to Calvin's youth. The dates in brackets are the revised dates of THL Parker in his John Calvin.

1509	Calvin born on 10 July in Noyon in Picardy, northern France. Henry VIII crowned King of England on 24 June.
1517	Martin Luther nails his 95 Theses to the door of the Castle Church in Wittenberg.
1523	(1520) Calvin enters the University of Paris.
1527/8	(1525/6) Calvin begins to study at the University of Orleans.
1529	Calvin begins to study at the University of Bourges.
1529–31	At some point Calvin experiences a 'sudden conversion'.
1531–3	Calvin continues his studies in Paris and Orleans.
1531	Calvin publishes his Commentary on Seneca's *De Clementia.*
1533	Calvin has to flee Paris in the wake of Nicolas Cop's Rectoral Address.
1533–34	Calvin wanders between Claix near Angouleme, Poiters, Nerac, Orleans and Paris. During this period he publishes *Psychpannychia.*
1534	The Incident of the Placards on 18 October after which Calvin flees first to Strasbourg.
1535	Calvin moves on to Basel.
1536	The first edition of the *Institutes* published in Basel.
1536	In March Calvin visits Ferrara in Italy.
1536	Calvin returns to Basel and Paris.
1536	Spending a night in Geneva Calvin is challenged by William Farel to stay and help him.
1536	on 10 November Calvin's programme for reformation presented to the Geneva city authorities.
1538	Calvin, Farel and Courauld are expelled from Geneva in April. Calvin goes to live in Basel.
1539	Calvin settles in Strasbourg as pastor of the French congregation.
1540	Calvin marries Idelette de Bure.
1541	Calvin returns to Geneva on 13 September.
1541	The *Ecclesiastical Ordinances* presented by Calvin to the city authorities.
1548	Idelette dies on 29 March.
1548	Theodore de Beze (Beza) arrives in Geneva.
1553	Michael Servetus executed on 27 October.
1553–58	During the reign of Mary Tudor in England many Protestants come to live in Geneva, including John Knox.
1558	The city authorities agree to establish the Geneva Academy.
1559	The Academy opened on 5 June.
1559	The final Latin edition of the *Institutes* published.
1562–63	The first War of Religion breaks out in France after the massacre of Protestants at Vassy.
1563	The Academy building is completed.
1564	Calvin dies on 27 May.

Author

Kenneth Brownell is the minister of East London Tabernacle Baptist Church in London. Born and raised in the United States he has a BA from Harvard University and a Ph.D. in modern history from the University of St. Andrews in Scotland. Dr. Brownell trained for the ministry at the London Theological Seminary where he now teaches modern church history. He is married to Alison, a physician, and they have two children, Katherine and Robert.

Acknowledgements

There are a number of people I would like to acknowledge and thank for their helpful comments and advice : Dr. Alan Clifford, Prof. Paul Helm, Mrs. Valerie Offord and Prof. Paul Wells. I would particularly like to thank Dr. Tony Lane of the London School of Theology for not only reading and commenting on the text, but also for giving me his time and access to his collection of photographs. Thanks to Steve Taylor, the librarian of the Evangelical Library, for his help. I also owe thanks to the series editor, Brian Edwards, for his immense patience and good will. Thanks too to Amanda Anderson for stepping in at a critical moment and sorting out many of the photographs. Three members of my church are owed thanks: Jeannine Herbert for helping on French accents; Winston Mattis for help with some photographs; and Norbert Boukero for helping on the visit to Noyon. I also want to thank East London Tabernacle Baptist Church, which it is my immense privilege to serve as pastor, for allowing me the time to write this book and bearing with my enthusiasm for Calvin. Last but not least I want to thank my wife Alison and our children, Kate and Rab, for their love and patience. To them I dedicate this book.

Picture acknowledgements

Steven Barlow: pages 32 (the Alps), 42 (Calvin's pulpit), 73 (St. Pierre), 83 (St. Pierre), 88 (interior of the Auditoire).

Robert Brownell: page 108 (Woodstock Congregational Church).

Tony Lane: pages 15 (Salle de Thèses), 18 (Calvin's first book), 23 (Church of the Mathurins), 25 (Calvin's tower), 45 (1536 Institutes), 46 (1559 Institutes), 47 (French Institutes), 62 (council minute), 67 (Reply to Sadoleto), 76 (Catechism), 101 (martyrdom of Ann de Bourg), 109 (Institutes).

Meeter Centre for Calvin Studies, Calvin College, Grand Rapids, Michigan: page 77 (Holbein portrait).

Musée Calvin, Noyon, France: pages 61 (portrtait of Idelette de Bure), 104 (portrait of Calvin).

Musée historique de la Réformation et Bibliothèque calvinienne, Genève. Exposé au Musée international de la Réforme, Genève (MHR). Musée international de la Réforme, Genève (MIR): pages 4 (Calvin at 53), 22 (young Calvin), 27 (candlestick cartoon), 38 (Froment preaching), 70 (elephant cartoon), 87 (cartoon of Calvin), 92 (candlestick cartoon) (Calvin's cup), 102, 105 (Calvin's meeting with colleagues for the last time), 122 (International Museum of the Reformation), page 119 (Geneva Academy).

Further Reading

T. Beza. *The Life of John Calvin* (Evangelical Press)

B. Cottret. *Calvin—A Biography* (T&T Clark)

P. Helm. *Calvin—A Guide for the Perplexed* (T&T Clark)

A. McGrath. *John Calvin* (Lion)

R. Reymond. *John Calvin—His Life & Influence* (Mentor)

H.Selderhuis. *John Calvin* (IVP)

W. Walker. *John Calvin* (Mentor)

Day One Audio Books

If you would like to download this John Calvin Travel Guide as an audio book please go to www.dayone.co.uk and click on Audio Books. Also available as an audio book: *Travel with William Tyndale* and *Travel with Billy Graham*.

DAY ONE TRAVEL GUIDES

The Day One Travel Guide series introduces our Christian heritage through people and places that have been influential in the history of western civilization and far beyond. They introduce the lives of great Christian leaders, past and present, and tour lands and cities with a strong biblical connection. They are written by authors who are specialists in their subject. Attractively produced with around 150 informative drawings and photographs. A tour guide to introduce the places associated with the subject. Equally valuable for the armchair traveler they bring people and places alive.

- **PLACES OF INTEREST**
- **PACKED WITH COLOUR PHOTOS**
- **CLEAR ILLUSTRATED MAPS**
- **GREAT GIFT IDEA**
- **128 PAGES**

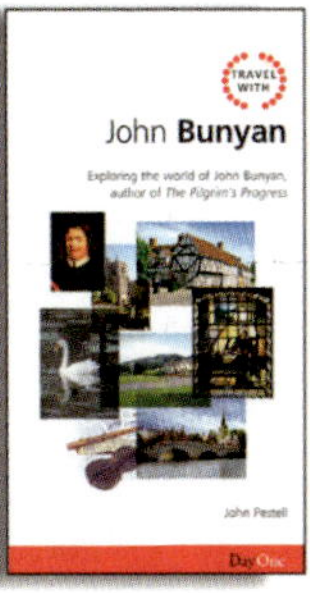
TRAVEL WITH
John Bunyan
Exploring the world of John Bunyan, author of The Pilgrim's Progress
John Pestell
Day One

TRAVEL WITH
CH Spurgeon
In the footsteps of the 'Prince of Preachers'
Clive Anderson
Day One

TRAVEL WITH
William Booth
Founder and first General of The Salvation Army
Jim Winter
Day One

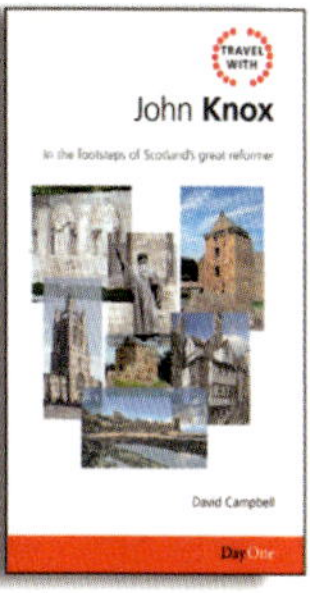
TRAVEL WITH
John Knox
In the footsteps of Scotland's great reformer
David Campbell
Day One

TRAVEL THROUGH
Oxford
City of saints, scholars and dreaming spires
Andrew Atherstone
Day One

TRAVEL THROUGH
Cambridge
City of beauty, reformation and pioneering research
David Berkley
Day One

TRAVEL THROUGH
Egypt
Land of Moses, monuments and mummies
Clive and Amanda Anderson
Day One

TRAVEL THROUGH
Israel
Land of promise, faith and beauty
Paul Williams and Clive Anderson
Day One

Through The
British Museum
with the Bible
Brian Edwards
Clive Anderson
Day One

TRAVEL WITH
The Martyrs
of Mary Tudor
The burning of Protestants during England's 'reign of terror'
Andrew Atherstone
Day One

TRAVEL WITH
Martyn Lloyd-Jones
Philip Eveson
Day One

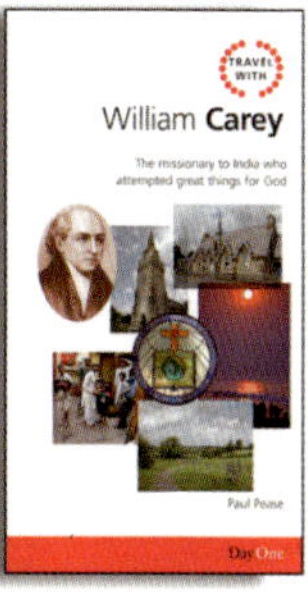
TRAVEL WITH
William Carey
The missionary to India who attempted great things for God
Paul Pease
Day One

TRAVEL WITH
William Tyndale
England's greatest Bible translator
Brian H Edwards
Day One

TRAVEL WITH
William Wilberforce
History's great social reformer
OLD PALACE YARD SW1
Kevin Belmonte
Day One

TRAVEL WITH
CS Lewis
The creator of Narnia and the most-quoted Christian of the 20th Century
Ronald W Bresland
Day One

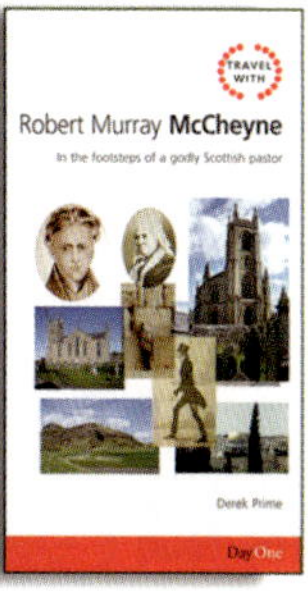
TRAVEL WITH
Robert Murray McCheyne
In the footsteps of a godly Scottish pastor
Derek Prime
Day One

FOOTSTEPS OF THE PAST

A series of children's activity books twinned with the Travel Guides

ROMANS, GLADIATORS AND GAMES
In the British Museum, explore the Roman world of the first Christians.

KINGS, PHARAOHS AND BANDITS
In the British Museum, explore the world of Abraham to Esther.

WILLIAM TYNDALE
He was threatened, hunted, betrayed and killed so that we could have the Bible in English

JOHN BUNYAN
How a hooligan and solidier became a preacher, prisoner and famous writer

WILLIAM CAREY
The story of a country boy and shoe mender whose big dreams took him to India

WILLIAM BOOTH
The troublesome teenager who changed the lives of people no one else would touch

C S LEWIS
The story of one of the world's most famous authors who sold over a hundred million books

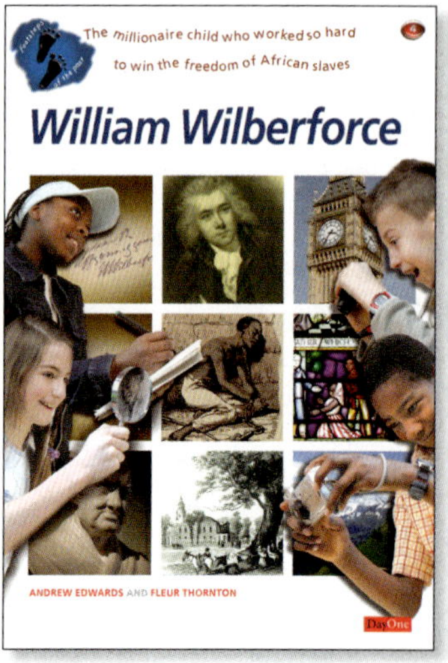

WILLIAM WILBERFORCE
The millionaire child who worked so hard to win the freedom of African slaves.

Permission is given to copy the activity pages and associated text for use as class or group material

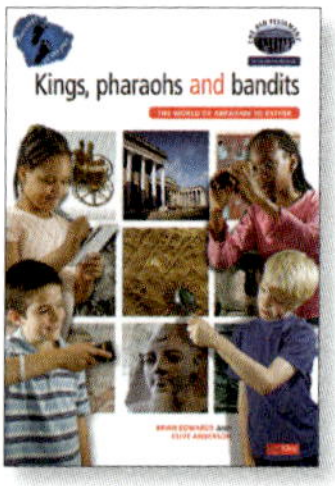